Amyotrophic Lateral Sclerosis ___

an *Amazing* *Love Story*

To Pat.

The Journey "Still"
Continues — — —

Peggy ✓ Jerry RIP
9/23/12

✝

Wendy

Amyotrophic Lateral Sclerosis ___

an Amazing Love Story

BEVERLY JACOBSON

Library of Congress Control Number: 2012904971
ISBN: Hardcover   978-1-4691-8526-2
                  Softcover   978-1-4691-8525-5
                  Ebook   978-1-4691-8527-9

NOTE: Biblical Quotations are from the New Revised Standard Version (NRSV), The New International Study Version (NIV) and the Max Lucado 3:16, New Century Version (NCV).

This book was printed in the United States of America.

To order additional copies of this book, contact:
Xlibris Corporation
1-888-795-4274
www.Xlibris.com
Orders@Xlibris.com
110596

Contents

In memory of my mother
Alice Helling Stearns
1911-1999

She endured with gentle dignity and grace
The ravages of Amyotrophic Lateral Sclerosis

This book is also prayerfully dedicated to the victims of ALS and their loved
ones. May you know God's presence and steadfast love as together you face this
deadly disease with commitment, courage, and love.

Beverly Jacobson

$\mathcal{A}$cknowledgements

$\mathcal{F}$irst of all, **to God Be the Glory!** *This book would not have been written without the promptings of the Holy Spirit nudging me along to tell the love story of Peggy and Jerry Weygandt.*

It's not that they are so different from others who have this deadly disease or the loved ones who care for them to the end. Rather, it is on behalf of all those folks who without any special recognition bravely face such an incredible death defying challenge and their dedicated care givers that I wrote this little book. The Weygandt's story is your story, too.

A special thanks to Amy and Duane Lingenfelter who have been faithful friends and encouragers. Amy for editing this little book and Duane, the computer whiz, who helped me know just enough to input the story on my laptop.

First United Methodist Church of Allen is a family oriented congregation that embraces all people and members truly do love and care for one another. My special thanks to all the members and pastors, especially The Rev. Todd Harris, The Rev. June Franck, and The Rev. Brian McPherson for sharing their observations.

My appreciation goes to David Franck and all the dear folks of Harmony Class who so generously offered love, care and information to tell this story. I appreciate Dr. Jaya R. Triviti, associate professor of Neurology, University of Texas Southwestern Medical Center for taking time to speak to me about her patient, Jerry, and his terminal illness, Amyotrophic Lateral Sclerosis. Thanks to the leaders and participants in the ALS Plano support group and all those friendly people in the Red River Rover's Recreational Vehicle Club.

Lee and Maureen Bowman have poured out their love and their energy in aiding his mother and step-father through these tough times. I am grateful for the Bowman's input and to all the brothers who care for Jerry and Peggy.

My beloved husband, Lowell Jacobson, was most supportive! He offered love, encouragement, insight, advice and took over meal preparation and household chores so I could spend hours on end writing, re-writing, arranging and re-arranging the chapters in this book.

Beverly Jacobson

Introduction

I first met Jerry and Peggy Weygandt (Pronounced Why—Ant) in 2007 at a church potluck Christmas Party in the First United Methodist Church of Allen, Texas.

He was in a wheelchair and she was quietly attending to his needs all the while both of them were happily chatting away with a group of friends. We were new to the church and had recently joined the Sunday morning class that the Weygandts also attended. My husband, Jake, and Jerry hit it off that night and talked and talked about the adventures of owning and traveling in motor homes.

We soon became part of a Sunday lunch bunch that included Jerry and Peggy. The more I observed the pair, the more it seemed I was to write their love story. And, so began our deepening friendship. We socialized together and also met for interviews, usually in the parlor of their modest home in Plano, Texas. Over the ensuing years, I met with some of the couple's family members, their church and RV friends, pastors and a large circle of associates.

There were many times when I wondered if Jerry would live to see the day his and Peggy's love story would be published. There were other times, as Jerry went from crisis-to-crisis, that I began to think my friend was somehow related to the "Energizer Bunny" or the Timex watch that *"takes a lickin' but keeps on tickin'"* because he just keeps bouncing back from death's door.

As a former daily newspaper features writer and editor, I saw the potential impact their inspiring story could have on others faced with a terminal illness. They do not despair but remain upbeat and hold fast to their faith.

The project began in the fall of 2008 with the writing of the first chapter, "The Challenge." At that point, Jerry was in a rather ordinary wheelchair and still had a bit of strength in his thumb to operate the toggle on the right arm of the chair to move it forward. His spindly legs could hold his body up-right to take a few shuffled steps to position himself to get into or out of the couple's regular van. When standing, his arms would dangle helplessly at his sides and his head would bob forward to rest his chin on his chest. He reminded me of a penguin.

As I write this, it is now December of 2011, and over the past few years I have observed Jerry's body give out; but I have yet to see him give up in to despondency. He is now bed ridden and cannot breathe on his own. It's been nearly a year since he's tasted food. He is fed by a feeding tube directly into his stomach. But that mind of his is still acutely keen and while he is now unable to talk, his shaggy eyebrows and piercing brown eyes leave no doubt about his emotions or what he wants to express!

Once again, we have come around to the annual Christmas Party. It was held at the church on December 2, 2011. There was a group of close to 50 senior citizens in attendance. We sat in a square arrangement of tables decorated in red and green with holiday candles and ornaments for centerpieces. There was a decorated Christmas tree atop a round table set in the center of the square with presents arranged all around the tree and on the floor; gifts for the Allen Community Outreach annual Christmas drive for needy children.

Folks were chatting and laughing in a festive mood. A hand held microphone was being handed around for people to share special Christmas memories of bygone years.

In the midst of the frivolity, everything stopped and all eyes turned to Peggy when her cell phone sounded. She quickly went to the far end of the multi-purpose room to take the call. We saw tears spill down Peggy's reddening face. Pastor June Franck quickly went to comfort her.

The room went silent.

It was as if everyone drew in a collective breath and held it.

We expected it could be news that Jerry had died.

The two women came back into the room to say they would be going to see Jerry because his oxygen levels were falling rapidly and the caregiver wanted Peggy to hurry home.

Someone said, "Let's pray right now!"

The group bowed and Kathryn Childress, the party organizer, prayed out loud.

She was interrupted by the sound of Peggy's cell phone.

Jerry's oxygen levels had begun to rise again.

The emergency was past!

The next morning I went to visit Jerry in his hospital bed at home. I was delivering several handwritten pages of personal greetings from church friends.

His body looked like that of a frail little boy. His weight is now less than 120 pounds. The skin on his motionless hands felt as soft as a baby's; signs of the loving care he receives from Peggy when she applies soothing aloe lotions.

What crossed my mind was here is a man who supposedly is on his last days and as his body is diminishing, he still resembles a strong lion with his hair combed back like the animal's mane and his bushy eyebrows shadow piercing, fierce brown eyes.

I offered my greeting and then looked past the patient to the wall behind his bed. There hangs a sign that says it all:

"Some people might think I am lucky . . .
. . . I think I am blessed that I am still here."

I wondered how Jerry felt about his approaching death.

He mouthed the words, "I'm ready."

He is ready to die.

However, Peggy struggles with letting go.

Peggy has let me know that her husband desires to see "The Book" finished before he dies.

So, I encouraged him to "Hang in there!"

The story, Jerry likes to call "The Journey" opens with an observation of how he appeared to me in the fall of 2008.

"My soul will boast in the Lord;
let the afflicted hear and rejoice."
Psalm 34:2

The Challenge

He can't walk.

He has trouble holding up his head.

He can't use his arms or hands.

He can't feed himself.

He can't dress himself.

He can't even wipe his nose.

But he still can smile.

He still can think.

He still can talk.

He still can joke around.

He can be glad, sad, happy or angry.

He still can and does influence, inspire and make a difference in other people's lives.

He still actively gives of himself to his marriage, family, church, friends, and community.

He hasn't hugged his wife in years, yet his eyes do so every time he looks at her.

He still is Jerry!

He is Jerry Weygandt of Plano, Texas. He is a man who has been living under a death sentence for nearly a decade. He has ALS, amyotrophic lateral sclerosis, a terminal illness also known as Lou Gehrig's disease.

And, this senior citizen will tell you, he is a better Jerry today than the one he was before he contracted this death sentence illness. He likes this Jerry better.

"I've learned so much—patience, loving, letting go of control, trusting God," Jerry mused as he relaxed in his wheelchair at home and talked about his illness.

"I used to be very demanding, hot tempered and controlling," he described himself as a matter of fact.

"Now, I am totally dependent on the goodness of others, and I have learned how kindness makes for peace and goodness in life."

Jerry was diagnosed with ALS after many frustrating years seeking answers to the mystery of his worsening debilitating condition.

His variety of ALS is known as BAD or Brachial Amyotrophic Dysplasia.

". . . and that's good!" Jerry said with a grin.

UTSW Medical Center

In an office interview, with his doctor, Jaya R. Triveti, an associate professor of Neurology in the Department of Neurology at the University of Texas Southwestern Medical Center in Dallas, she explained to me that BAD is a slower moving variant form of the disease Amyotrophic Lateral Sclerosis.

The neurologist explained that some people suffering from ALS die within months or a year from their diagnosis because muscle deterioration causes them to rapidly lose use of limbs and bodily functions, including speech.

"The brain is the last to go," she offered, sadly.

Jerry's BAD form of this deadly disease was diagnosed in 2003.

There is no easy way to give a person such a gruesome diagnosis.

However, the man who was once a handsome, vigorous, six feet tall and 185 pounds, physically fit guy with a cocky 'I-can-do-anything' kind of attitude said he somehow felt relief to hear the diagnosis. He and his petite, 5 feet 3 inches tall, adoring wife had spent years in frustration going from doctor-to-doctor looking for answers as to why Jerry's strength continued to dissipate. Why was his body shutting down? Why was he losing use of his arms and legs?

Jerry said finally getting an answer meant more than hearing that it meant he was going to die.

Because? He was asked.

"Well, aren't we all (going to die)?" he responded with a smug smile.

Lou Gehrig's disease

Jerry is asked if he identifies with the famous, beloved New York Yankees baseball player Lou Gehrig, who died of ALS in 1941 and will forever be identified with the insidious deadly disease.

Gehrig is remembered for describing himself as "the luckiest man on the face of the earth." He spoke those words in Yankee Stadium in a gracious acceptance speech on his last day with teammates, including Babe Ruth, and ball fans, all in shock with the news of his terminal illness. Gehrig's manager presented the ball player with a trophy recognizing all he had meant to the team and his fans.

Does Jerry ever think of himself as "lucky?"

He let out a "harrumph," cocked his head slightly to consider the question, and after a pause said, "Look at my wife, my family, friends and all who care for me. Yes. I suppose you could call me lucky."

"My body may have to deal with the deadly disease ALS but, **A—L—S—does—not—have—me!**" He says this slowly; emphatically.

He went on to explain, "To be able to live with a diagnosis of a terminal illness you have to be able to exist one day at a time. If you waste time worrying about what is going to happen, you won't be able to live today,"

That's how Jerry and Peggy approach their life together. They make the disease their daily challenge.

"We are not going to let ALS defeat our enjoyment of each other or the joy of living," says Jerry.

"Our life is like a dance," adds the soft spoken Peggy.

It's a dance only for the couple and they believe they will go on together long after the music fades away.

"You turned my wailing into dancing;
You removed my sackcloth and clothed me with joy
that my heart may sing to you and will not be silent.
O Lord God, I will give you thanks forever."
Psalm 30: 11-12

He Bites. She Bites.

They are something to behold.

It is almost as if they live inside each other's heads.

He says they speak words with their eyes.

To the observer it is like no words are necessary.

It's a graceful, intimate, silent dance of love known only to the couple. Their communication is so seamless that others scarcely notice that she is feeding him.

He sits next to her with his wheelchair up to a round restaurant table.

He bites.

She bites.

He talks.

She talks.

Others join in the table talk.

Back and forth with no hesitation the conversation travels around the table. The chatter gets louder and louder as others file into the restaurant.

It's Sunday morning.

Jerry and Peggy Weygandt, like a lot of married couples, are out for lunch with friends.

They are engaged in what they usually do after attending worship services and an adult discussion class at First United Methodist Church in Allen, Texas. They go out to eat.

They break bread together at one or another of the restaurants in the neighborhood.

They chat.

They joke.

They laugh.

They talk about the fabric of their lives.

Joys.

Hurt feelings.

Good news and bad news.

Disappointments

Secret desires.

The group of six and sometimes more is no different from the hundreds of after church gatherings in restaurants all around the country.

He bites.

She bites.

They laugh.

They talk.

The man in the wheelchair welcomes the stares and sideways glances of strangers.

Jerry sees his helplessness, except for his mind and strong voice, as his life's purpose. He wants other handicapped people confined to wheelchairs to see him out and about and be encouraged to do the same.

Peggy agrees. She also will tell you it is *their* mission!

They are in this together.

That might astonish some able bodied as well as some disabled people. Why would anyone in a right mind want to call a terminal illness a mission, a blessing?

Jerry and his devoted wife have come to believe that is exactly what their lives are about.

They believe their spiritual purpose is to help others to see God's love in hardships. They want others with physical disabilities and even terminal illnesses to hold on to hope. They want to inspire others, with God's help, to "keep on, keeping on," as Jerry would say, "for as long as they are able, for as long as they live."

"God didn't put me in this chair!" he says firmly. "My disease did. But for as long as I am able, I can and I will be a witness to how God uses this bad situation for good!" His brown eyes show firm resolve. He looks straight into the listener's eyes when he speaks.

In measured, determined words he goes on to say, "I want to be seen as capable of contributing to society. I want others with disabilities to know that they are loved by God and worthy of dignity, respect, attention, and consideration as much as others who are able bodied."

His eyes never leave the listener as he emphasizes his dedication to a mission to be seen as one that the Bible calls "blessed to be a blessing."

"My illness doesn't mean God has abandoned me. It means God is with me in this experience and offers me strength and comfort to endure to serve others in a special way," said Jerry.

But let us not get ahead of the story. The next several chapters will take you back in Jerry's past so you can see the making of the man and the steely determination that has served him well as he faces a deadly disease that robs him of the use of his body.

so that by it, you may grow up in your salvation,
"Like newborn babies crave pure spiritual milk,
now that you have tasted that the Lord is good."
1 Peter 2:3

Lessons learned on a Milking Stool

*A*ttributes like:

- Determination.
- Hard work.
- Tenacity.
- The drive to stick with something until you figure out.
- The grit to "hang in there" against the odds.

Those characteristics didn't just arrive in Jerry at the same time as the sinister movements of ALS began taking over his body.

Those strong qualities were building strength in Jerry from the start. He was born April 14, 1940 with Rh-negative blood factor. He sees that as the beginning of his tenacity to survive.

"They changed my blood when I was born," said Jerry, the youngest of three children. He has a brother Laurel Jr., four years older, and a sister, Donna Kay, two years older.

"Dad worked for B.F. Goodrich in Akron driving a fork lift. We had a gentleman's farm of five acres in Copley, Ohio so we always had a milk cow, pigs and a big garden. The land was divided between field corn and pasture. We all worked hard. Mom stayed home and took care of us kids and cracked the whip," said Jerry, enjoying the memories of his youth.

He shouldered man-sized responsibilities from a young age. He got a rifle for his 14th birthday and spent a lot of time hunting in the big woods behind the house.

"I loved hunting," Jerry said during an interview recalling his boyhood.

"It was not unusual for me to go anywhere in the woods and have the dogs with me to kick up rabbits or to sneak up on woodchucks," he said with a grin.

But the days of carefree youth were shortened when his father announced the family was going to do the work to build a house on their property.

He proudly described how he nailed down sub-flooring and plastered walls.

"There is a picture of me pointing to my older brother, and telling him what to do." Jerry chuckled.

"I think I did much of the work. The house was finished when I was in eighth grade. It was the first time we had indoor plumbing and then in less than a year the house was sold."

The family moved about 20 miles away to a scraggly 70 acres farm, purchased for $15 thousand near Sharon Center, Ohio. Jerry, just starting high school, faced more hard work. His older brother and sister were no longer living at home.

"All of a sudden, we are in the dairy farming business," Jerry recalled.

His father worked the night shift, 11 pm.-to-7 am. and that left some farm work to the schoolboy. "Dad had taught me how to hand milk a cow." That was when Jerry was a seventh grader living on the previous farmstead.

What did Jerry the teenager think about as he was sitting on a three legged milking stool day after day, dawn and dusk, milking an expanding herd of dairy cows?

With a sheepish grin, Jerry admitted that his answer was not something spiritual his questioner may have been seeking. Rather, he allowed it most likely was about Marjie, a skinny farm girl with auburn hair in a ponytail, who lived up the road. She often pitched in to help Jerry with farm chores. That is until the time he urged a recalcitrant cow to move on by hitting the cow on the rump with a shovel.

"The cow jumped and slipped on manure and that sent a fresh pie sailing into the air landing in the newly arriving Marjie's face!"

While Jerry is proud of his ability as a teenaged boy to handle "One hundred percent of the responsibility" for a herd of cows that grew to 50 head, there may be a twinge of regret for some lost youth adventures.

"I felt total exhilaration at being in control of everything I did," he said. That included the rush he got from swooping basketballs into the hoop in front of a roaring crowd at high school games.

"I had to give it up."

He had gotten good at the sport from practicing on the basketball hoop hung on the barn. He was a starting team player as a junior on his high school basketball team. He quit playing his senior year because of "the continual harassment at home over farm work." He saw his work was vital to keep the farm operating.

"It was a little disconcerting that I got so good at something and then had to give it up."

But Jerry will tell you something learned as a boy with a man's responsibilities, "You don't get anything or get anywhere without hard work!"

An A grades student in high school Jerry said he "Never took a book home. It was all done at school with a heavy class load."

He graduated in 1958 from Highland High School, Medina, Ohio and was already committed to service with the U.S. Army Reserves

"I thought of myself as indestructible!"

*"Do not store up for yourselves treasures on earth,
where moth and rust destroy, and where thieves break in and steal"*
Matthew 6:19

All Systems Go

Wiping farm dirt off his shoes, the high school graduate took off for six weeks of basic training with the U.S. Army at Fort Jackson in Columbia, S. C.

Jerry had signed up for the military in January of his senior year. He had agreed to six months active duty and then seven and one half years of service in the Army Reserves.

"There wasn't anything holding me back!" said Jerry who began active duty as a Private (E-1).

"I thought military life was ok," he said about the short time he actively served. He even gave some thought to continuing on active duty to become a paratrooper.

But there was something calling him home. It was a pretty little brown haired, 17 years old girl, named Amy who worked as a waitress in a little café that Jerry frequented.

"She always waited on me," he revealed with a shy grin.

He said the hard working teenager came from a poor family and was obliged to care for her two younger brothers.

He left active duty, got a job at a farm and garden store and dated shyly flirtatious waitress.

They married in September of 1959, four months after she graduated from high school.

26

Their first son, Gerald Dean Weygandt Jr., was born February 28, 1960, and soon after the new family headed west seeking their fortune with Jerry feeling "all powerful" behind the wheel of his brand new 1959 Pontiac "muscle car" two-door sedan.

"Oh, it was fast!" exclaimed the man sitting in a wheelchair being interviewed about his earlier life.

"I thought of myself as indestructible. There wasn't anything holding me back," he recalled.

He and Amy and the baby settled into a small apartment near her sister in the Los Angeles area.

"Jobs were easy to get and so I worked several," said Jerry.

He worked as a mechanic for a big nursery dealer in Monrovia. He maintained the fleet of jeeps that transported stock to various customers. He was proud of the fact that he was the only one who could drive semi-trucks into and out of the mechanic's garage to check them out without unhitching their trailers.

"The semi-drivers couldn't do that," he said smugly.

But all his raw confidence and good paying jobs could not compete with the red smarting eyes and itching noses that came from the L.A. smog filled air. So, after a year, Jerry moved his family back to Wadsworth, Ohio and began to learn the electrician's trade.

Three more sons came along: Kevin, born on December 18, 1961, Greg, born May 24, 1963 and Eric, was born April 24, 1970.

Jerry put in long hours learning to be an electrician. He was as determined to be the best electrician on the job as he had been about excelling as a mechanic. He was willing to put in as many hours as needed to out-do any of the others.

"Nobody can beat you if you are Number One," said Jerry. He was sitting helplessly in a wheelchair, but enjoying the look back with pride to the days long ago when he felt strong and free and superiorly able.

He had learned to use his wits and be resourceful as a farm boy and that served him well again as he applied himself to the electrical trade. He spent the next twelve years building his skills on the job.

"I was good at what I did! I could be in the foundry in the morning covered in dirt and in the afternoon at a million dollar home in Akron and do both jobs well. I carried clean clothes in my truck and had a complete set of tools for foundry work and a complete set of tools to go anywhere else. I became the foundry expert, so if there was anything needed they would call and say, "Send Jerry."

He never did join the union.

He tells me, his interviewer, with a note of pride, that he was able to circumvent the union apprenticeship program and membership because he "knew more than anyone else."

"I worked for a number of contractors all at the same time," Jerry said.

When he wasn't at work, he spent time with his sons in Boy Scouts and sports, like baseball.

One senses, as the paralyzed man walks down memory lane, that the reliving is giving him new insights into his past life and actions. He is seeing now that he shared in the demise of his first marriage. His voice that started out with a sharp edge placing blame on his ex-wife softens as he goes into a lengthy explanation of his failed marriage.

"Amy got a job and that put us in another tax bracket," he tells me and with the dull tone of his voice, you would have expected to see him shrug his shoulders if he were able.

The couple grew apart.

They divorced.

Jerry vowed he would gain custody of all four of his sons. He and oldest son, Dean, moved into an apartment. Jerry stayed in touch with his three younger sons through the Boy Scouts.

And that's where the plot thickens in the fall of 1974 at a dinner where the Webelos were advancing to be full-fledged Boy Scouts. Jerry and his sons happened to sit at the same table as single parent, Peggy Bowman, and her two sons.

He knew her sons to be good boys from scouting. He felt attracted to their mother.

"Well, I still believed strongly that I could do anything I set my mind to and at that moment, I set my mind to pursue Peggy and marry her!"

"Fear God and keep his commandments,
for this is the whole duty of man."
Ecclesiastes 12:13

Scouting Around

With all those Boy Scouts, Jerry and his four sons and Peggy and her two, there were plenty of occasions for the adults to see each other.

After all, Jerry was the conscientious scout leader and Peggy was the single mother doing her best to make sure her sons were receiving discipline and a strong healthy male influence in the absence of their father.

She saw Jerry as a strong, tall, dark and handsome man with the heart and energy to inspire healthy virtues in young men. He saw her as a slender, lovely, pretty, brown eyed, brown haired petite woman with steely determination and a caring heart to do right for her sons.

For this interview, as with most throughout the four years of compiling information, Peggy is seated so that her eyes are on Jerry. She listens and occasionally interjects a few words from her side of their story. She adores this man and quietly and gracefully gives her all to attending to his well-being.

At this point in time, November of 2008, Jerry is still in a rather ordinary wheelchair. It has a ditty bag hanging on the back with items such as eye drops, a small hand towel, drinking straws, and tissues that Peggy will pick up and surreptitiously use to attend to her husband's needs.

She just does it. She seems to intuitively know. He never seems to need to ask.

Peggy tells me she "had a different feeling deep down inside" the day Jerry came and joined the table where she and her boys were seated at that Boy Scout dinner.

The two single parents, each one hurting from divorce, found a commonality that led to more and more conversations and happy times spent together . . . often all eight of them!

The boys ranged in ages from 15, 14, 13, 13, 12 and 4.

At that time, the single father was in litigation with his former wife for custody of all four of his sons. He and Dean were often at Peggy's house around dinnertime to enjoy tasty home cooked meals.

"I never did ask Peggy to marry me," said Jerry.

Instead he asked her oldest son, Lee, who was age 15 at that time, and he readily gave permission.

With a chuckle, Jerry recalled how at that time his soon-to-be stepson responded, "Why not? You're over at our house all the time anyway!"

The couple's next hurdle was to figure out how they would house themselves and six boys!

With Jerry's carpentry and electrician skills they set out to turn the basement of her small 1950s style house into a master bedroom with bath and a family room area.

"The boys would have the upstairs," Peggy reported to the writer.

She went on to describe a snowy day, December 19, 1975, when they spoke their marriage vows with six boys present. They had more than a marriage to celebrate! Jerry had just won full custody of his four sons.

On their wedding night, the newlyweds had sent the six boys up the stairs to their bedrooms and then they started down the basement steps to their new quarters.

As they descended the steps, Greg, in a teasing, giggly, singsong voice said: "Good night! Have fun!"

And that sent off gales of laughter from the four older boys as they all raced up the steps to their rooms on the second floor.

This was the start of many adventures for this blended family.

"Sons are a heritage from the Lord, children a reward from him,
like arrows in the hands of a warrior are sons born in one's youth.
Blessed is the man whose quiver is full of them."
Psalm 127

Six Sons

Lee Bowman, now age 50, the oldest of those six sons in the blended family, now lives near his mother and step-father in Allen, Texas. He and his wife, Maureen are committed to helping their older parents. One fall day in 2009 both were at the Weygandt's Plano home up to their elbows in blue paint when I made an unexpected visit. They seemed delighted to take a break from the project of applying bright blue paint to the walls in the master bedroom.

Lee seemed pleased to pull up a chair and talk about those early days after his Mom married Jerry.

"I was the smallest in size of the older guys," said the jovial, ruddy faced man with a fringe of red hair circling his balding head.

"What I remember is that there was never enough food to go around," he said. "Mother was used to cooking for three, Mom, my younger brother Dwight, and me. Then with Jerry and his four sons, suddenly we were eight. If you wanted to have second helpings you had to eat fast or you would be left out."

The oldest of the newly formed band of brothers described how he would find a way to distract the other boys so that while they were doing something like gawking out the window to see the neighbor's "new car" that Lee talked about, he would be filling his plate with seconds.

Lee didn't recall much about the family attending church. Just that they did and it was always a part of their life. He said that his Mother and Jerry didn't talk to the boys so much about God as they lived by example.

A happy memory for the entire family was a vacation trip to the Grand Canyon taken the year after the couple married. Jerry and the five older boys hiked down the south rim and on up to the north rim while Peggy and Eric, then 5, drove around the canyon to meet them with their van.

"We did it in two days. It usually took three," said Lee, exhibiting youthful enthusiasm that came with the memory.

He described his new step-father as being, "Very robust."

"We looked up to him. He was a task master but we all admired him," said Lee.

The overnight camp found the six adventurers "sleeping on a big, flat rock."

"We got up before the sun . . . to get off that hard rock . . . and then we hiked on to the north rim."

You see the glow of a teenage boy's pride as the man describes how he had been given the responsibility to go on ahead with all the supplies.

"But when the others didn't show up, I backtracked because they were not arriving as soon as expected at the next camp site.

Lee described how when he reconnected with Jerry and the other four boys, he saw they had stopped, exhausted from the blazing hot sun and hard climb.

"I gave them some raisins and cookies and then we all made it the rest of the way."

There was admiration in his voice as Lee described his step-father as "a strong man, aware and confident about doing whatever needed to be done."

The attentive oldest son gulped and choked back tears when he was asked what he thought about his step-father slowly dying from a terminal illness.

He looked down, sighed, slowly shook his head from side to side and almost inaudibly said, "I just don't go there. I don't want to think about that."

". . . have genuine mutual love,
love one another deeply from the heart."
1 Peter 1:22b

Building a Partnership

*T*heirs was a binding partnership from day one of the marriage. Jerry and Peggy knew they had to present a united front for those six sons. They were all entering into a new blended family in which each one of them bore scars of emotional pain from the previous failed marriages and shattered hopes and dreams.

The Weygandt sons still had time with their mother and the Bowman boys saw their dad. But, they were also about building new family bonds.

"We knew we needed to be up front, together and intentional in our relationship with the boys, with each other and our work," said Jerry.

"We learned from the past mistakes and had such a feeling of gratitude for the chance to love again and make a go of it," said Peggy.

By the time they married, Jerry was making a good living working for an electrical contractor. He had started out as the driver of a service truck and learned electrician's craft from observing his boss on the job.

Jerry says he got so good at the job that the business grew. He worked well and fast.

"I learned to climb poles so I could go out and finish a service call in one day while the general contractor would take three or four days to do the same kind of job."

Jerry boasts he was the main electrician on a million dollar building job with "no competition".

His brown eyes flash with pride as he recalls, "I designed it, sold the project and collected!"

Jerry enjoyed describing how the "collecting" took a bit of finessing on his part. He was with his boss sitting in the customer's swank mahogany furnished office and saw the man hand his check to pay the bill to Jerry's boss.

"I saw the boss' face go white. The check was for, say $75 thousand less than we had billed for," Jerry recalled.

"I looked back at the owner, took the check from my boss' hand and brought it to the owner's desk and said, "My boss doesn't deserve this. The job was done on time. You were sent a bill for the full amount owed, and we expect to leave here with that."

Jerry reported that the man grimaced and opened his mahogany desk drawer and pulled out a check with the appropriate amount.

"I handed it to my boss and we left."

That Christmas marked the end of Jerry working for somebody else. When he opened his Christmas bonus check and saw it was only for $50 he told his long time employer, "Meet your new competition!"

That tenacity has stuck with Jerry right up to the present day.

It was with him the day of the fall.

But I'm getting ahead of the story . . .

*"He put a new song in my mouth
a song of praise to our God."*
Psalm 40:3

Taking Care of Business

From the get-go, Jerry and Peggy say they were a team, raising sons and running a business. The competition was fierce for electrical contractors in Wadsworth, Ohio area.

He ran the electrical business. She managed the office and on the side, also operated a retail computer store helping people design personal computer systems, selling the components, and teaching 'how to' classes.

The electrical contracting business grew to 20 employees as Jerry pulled in successful bids from big companies and government offices including the U.S. Postal Service.

"Hard work has it benefits," the man in the wheelchair reflected. "I learned you don't get anywhere without hard work."

He stopped talking as if he was taking in what he had just heard himself say. When he began to speak again, his words were uttered softly, slowly, more to himself than to his listeners.

"Maybe that *is* the story of my life. Hard work might also have been my downfall."

Jerry described how he developed an edge in the competition by developing the skill to read upside down to spy the numbers being bid by others and then he came in under that bid to get the electrical job.

"If it was for say $10 grand, I would offer $999 thousand," he said.

Then he would go one better by telling the customer that if he were to accept Jerry's bid right then, he would have the contract on the potential buyer's desk before the end of the day.

That's where the pair excelled working together. Jerry would go out to his truck, call his wife and business partner and in less than an hour, he would be back in the man's office with a contract ready for his signature."

When the astonished buyer would ask how Jerry got the contract to him so fast he would proudly say, "That's how we do business."

It was those successful bidding experiences that taught Jerry an important lesson he still uses today. Since his illness and confinement to a wheelchair, he has not shrunk from making his and Peggy's needs known. It's something they urge others with disabilities and their caregivers to do. Jerry believes most folks are pleased to be asked for help. He thinks it makes others feel good to be able to offer assistance to someone who is handicapped.

"I've learned you can go ahead and ask," he said. "I've asked God for something or other people for something. If the answer is no, it doesn't bother me. I just figure they didn't want to or God didn't want it that way."

"But, often I find people are more than happy to accommodate your request. You just need to speak up and make your request known."

Good Business

Dwight Bowman, who lives in Ohio, knows about his step-father's strong work habits. He joined his mother and step-father in the computer side of the business in 1984.

"Jerry has an entrepreneurial spirit," Dwight wrote in an email to the interviewer. "He started two businesses. The first was his electrical business. The second was the computer business. Jerry saw early in the time of personal computers that they were going to be something worth getting involved with and started The Complete Computer House. I joined this business with him and my Mom and it started a career in technology for me," he wrote.

Snow Birds

When all six boys had left the nest, Jerry and Peggy began full time traveling in the early 1990s, first in a travel trailer, then in a fifth wheel trailer and later on in a Dutch Star motor home. They would follow the birds flight pattern traveling south in the winter and north in the summer picking up electrical jobs and other temporary work along their way.

"It was a wonderful time. We have been to every state in the U.S. except Maine, New Hampshire, Vermont, Connecticut, Rhode Island, Alaska and Hawaii," said Peggy.

". . . do not fear for I am with you, do not be afraid
for I am your God; I will strengthen you, I will help you,
I will uphold you with my victorious right hand."
Isaiah 41:10

The Fall

*L*ife was idyllic for the Weygandts over the next several years.
    The husband and wife team became full time RVers traveling across the country, sightseeing and going from job-to job. They made new friends with other folks like themselves who had adopted the nomadic lifestyle.

"We just loved it! We made so many good friends wherever we would go," Peggy told her interviewer.

"We never had trouble finding work. Once people saw what Jerry could do, they were glad to have him, and I was appreciated because of my computer knowledge and office management experience," she said.

Once again, the couple is settled in their living room for a two hour visit intended to fill in background details on their story as it leads to the diagnosis of Jerry having ALS, a terminal illness. Jerry's doctor says he has a slower advancing variety of the deadly disease. And, while medical science has yet to explain the cause and find a cure for Amyotrophic Lateral Sclerosis, Jerry thinks his terminal illness may somehow link back to his military service or to what happened on the electrical job he was doing for the New Hope Methodist Church in Elkhart, Indiana.

"It was July, 1995," says Jerry, slowly drawing in a breath.

I notice with his introductory words, Peggy's face has saddened. She lowers her head and casts teary eyes downward to her hands folded in her lap. This is not going to be an easy time for her. Her husband shows little emotion.

"We were in Elkhart, Indiana, and I happened to see this picture and a big article in the newspaper about some Methodists who were building a new church using mostly all volunteer labor. I didn't have anything else to do so I decided to stop by to see what was going on and maybe offer to help," Jerry said.

So, he donned his hard hat and headed out to find the building site.

"I saw people milling around doing various jobs, hammering, sawing, raising walls. There was a huge crane ready to lift the joist to the roof," he said. After a time of looking around, he introduced himself and chatted with the church's preacher who showed Jerry the blueprints for the 6,000 square foot facility under construction.

Jerry liked what he saw.

The next day, he returned to the building site and the preacher introduced him to the electrical contractor. The man hired Jerry on the spot to do the electrical work at the church.

Soon after, the Weygandts joined the New Hope Methodist Church and Jerry set to work to help get the building project done by Christmas.

"It was a Monday," he recalled.

None of the volunteers were at the building project because the men were on a Labor Day weekend retreat. Jerry didn't go because he was concerned about getting the electrical work completed that had been postponed because the mechanical contractor was late completing his part of the project.

The electrician described how the mechanical contractor had cut a four feet by six feet hole in the ceiling so his workers could get their equipment up into the attic. Jerry described how he had crossed over the hole many times doing his work. That morning, he was alone at the building site. He worked in a dark, cramped space on his hands and knees crawling his way from one end of the attic toward the other stapling low voltage cable for fire and security alarms.

When he reached the hole he stopped work.

He sat back on his haunches.

He wiped his brow.

"My back was to the opening in the floor. I stood up and turned around to take one step to the edge but that step put me to the middle of the hole and down I went."

He threw his arms out trying to grab a floor joist as he was rapidly hurtling through space.

He missed and crashed on his back on the concrete floor below.

Today, Jerry will tell you he believes an Angel traveled with him on that downward plunge.

"I could have died," he whispered.

". . . God will not fail you or forsake you."
Deut. 31:6

After the Fall

"*I* landed ten feet below on my back."

Jerry doesn't know how long he may have lay alone on the concrete floor.

No one else was on the job.

No one saw him fall.

He was alone in the building.

Everything was silent.

No one saw the sawdust and dust billow up around him when his body smashed to the concrete floor below.

He had no air power in his lungs to call for help.

"I'd open my mouth but couldn't make a sound," he recalled. "My chest felt like it was on fire."

Finally, another worker happened into the building and Jerry, in excruciating pain, was able with a raspy, faint breath to weakly cry for help.

The worker spotted Jerry's crumpled body on the ground. He turned and ran across the street to a pay phone to call for an ambulance. Cell phones had not yet come into popular use.

Jerry spent nine days in the hospital being treated for four broken ribs and a collapsed lung. He also had a broken neck, but that was not discovered until five years later.

"They never x-rayed above the neck," he said of that initial hospitalization in Elkhart, Indiana, after the accident.

There is no drama in the way Jerry speaks about the devastating accident. Perhaps it has become common place in the telling and retelling of the story over these ensuing years.

Jerry said he never fully recovered from that fall. While he did regain enough strength to briefly return to work, he needed an assistant to help do lifting, such as for tool boxes and ladders.
Peggy tears up as she interjects that Jerry was never again the strong, vigorous man he had been before the fall.

Jerry is telling this part of their story from his wheelchair. His arms rest helplessly on the chair arms. His feet are positioned on the chair's foot rests. His black Nikes will always look like new shoes because his feet are never going to take him anywhere.

Jerry wants people to know that he likes himself better the way he is now. He describes how he has a deeper sense of God, himself and his life's purpose today then he did when he was the outspoken, indestructible, handsome, physically fit, successful businessman in the trades for some 30 years.

While Jerry seems to have accepted his fate, Peggy struggles with her emotions. She tries to hold back tears. She does not like her husband to see her cry. While she is seated on the couch next to the interviewer, her attention is always riveted on her husband. She offers him sips of water through a straw in a glass for him to clear his throat, while he continued to expound on his side of their story.

He described how, as he was being loaded into the ambulance for the emergency trip to the Elkhart hospital, he asked the man who found him to please go to Peggy at her workplace and tell her what had happened and bring her to the hospital.

"It scared me to death!" said Peggy, taking in a big breath and twisting her fingers together.

"I was at work on a temporary job and another employee came and said someone was there to see me. My knees went weak when I heard there had been an accident and that Jerry had taken a fall and was going by ambulance to a hospital."

She said she relaxed after she saw Jerry and that he was awake and alert. That is until their pastor showed up.

"Then I was scared again because I thought there was something they (medical personnel) were not telling me," she said.

Many years have passed since his accident. Jerry has had a lot of time to look back at his steady decline into complete helplessness. He is asked, if he ever wonders why God would let such a horrible thing happen to him? Does he blame God for his misfortunes?

His eyebrows shot up like he'd taken a bullet to the chest.

"No!" He exclaimed with a sharp edge to his voice.

"I absolutely do not!" He said.

He seemed taken aback by the audacity of the question.

Then, his voice took on a thoughtful, yet firm resonance when he spoke again.

"Do I believe God can make something good out of a bad situation?"

"Yes," he responded, "I absolutely do!"

It continues to be a mystery as to what causes the deadly disease ALS, Amyotrophic Lateral Sclerosis. Jerry and Peggy wonder if the fall triggered something in his body that brought on the disease. Medical science more recently has linked the terminal illness to possibly something with the military. The US Veterans Administration is now treating anyone who served in the military who has been diagnosed with Amyotrophic Lateral Sclerosis. This has been a big help to the financially strapped Weygandts as you will see in the chapters to come.

Since Jerry sees his spiritual purpose to be one of enduring with grace this deadly illness, does he ever wish he would wake up some morning cured? Would he like to have his strong, vigorous, healthy body back?

"Of course," he replied. "But not if I had to let go of what I have learned about myself and God since becoming incapacitated. I believe God is using me in this chair to remind others that no matter their circumstances, God is with them and wants them to live the best life they can. God will never leave or forsake you, no matter what," he said.

"God has called me to sit helpless in this wheelchair for a reason. I am to set an example to encourage others to keep on living, with God's help, no matter what your circumstances are."

With a big smile, Jerry concluded this portion of our interview by saying, "My days for being free to move all about are ahead of me ___ in the life to come."

"For the gate is narrow and the road
is hard that leads to life."
Matthew 7:13

On the Road Again

Folks at New Hope United Methodist Church called Peggy, "The Cheerleader." They had observed her attentiveness and loving care for Jerry during the time he was in the Elkhart hospital and after they returned from rehabilitation work in a facility in Arlington, Texas.

"She was doing lots for me and for other people and making everybody feel good like she always does," said Jerry with an admiring look toward his beloved wife.

The couple exchange loving looks as he continued with their story.

"Our circumstances are different (than married couples without physical handicaps). I have it good. I have someone who thinks ahead, sees what needs to be done and gets it done. We understand each other," he said as tears gathered at the rims of his eyes.

"She is as committed as I am to getting the most out of life."

The couple ventured on the road again. It was September, 1997.

They loved the motor home lifestyle.

Now, however, it was Peggy's full responsibility to be the driver of their 38 foot long rig. It would be up to her to manage leveling the motor home, make sewer and electrical connections, and all the physical work procedures required to set up or break down camp.

"Jerry wasn't even able to hold a screw driver," she sadly recalled.

"We weren't getting any help that made any sense from doctor visits. We saw that it was time to get some answers."

At this point in the interview, Peggy inhaled deeply and then slowly exhaled. She was buying some time to compose her emotions before going on.

"So we came to Texas to find out what's wrong with Jerry."

They chose Plano to be near son, Lee and family, and to be seen at some of the best medical facilities in the nation.

Their first stop was to Texas Back Institute (TBI), an internationally acclaimed facility located in Plano.

"The doctor there gave Jerry a 17 percent impairment rating but had no explanation for the cause." Peggy recalled.

"He sent us to physical therapy and that's where we met Wendy, a TBI physical therapist. But after four visits, she didn't know what else to do (with no diagnosis) so we didn't go back again."

Jerry continued to decline. They returned to TBI and this time he was given a 39 percent impairment rating.

"So he keeps getting worse," said Peggy sadly shaking her head. She looks down at her hands as she continues to talk about the couple's fears and frustrations in the search for answers. During this time, they lived in an RV park. They made short trips with Red River Rovers Club.

"We were referred to a neurologist at University of Texas Southwestern Medical Center (UTSW) and that's when Jerry received a 49 percent impairment rating."

It was August 2003. Peggy had been laid off from her job with Man Power because of an economic downturn.

"Jerry was age 61 and I had just turned 65. It seemed to be the right time for me to collect Social Security and stay home and care for my dear husband."

After Peggy completed filling out a Social Security application, Jerry inquired about what it would take for him to get disability benefits. To their delight, Jerry was accepted immediately and that first social security disability check was retroactive to the first of the year.

At that time, Jerry was still managing to shuffle along slowly going for short distances. His arms would dangle at his sides because he had no strength to raise them. He was losing use of his hands as well.

The Weygandts bought their cozy home in Plano and turned their full energy to seeking answers for Jerry's failing health.

The news was bad and yet that was good ___ the Weygandts finally had the diagnosis of Amyotrophic Lateral Sclerosis. They knew what they were dealing with. They would not give in to the terminal illness but would live life to the fullest as best as they could for as long as they could.

And that is how the Weygandts came to renew an acquaintance with a physical therapist they first met after a doctor's visit some years past during a stop in Plano during their recreational vehicle travel adventures.

"Therefore encourage one another and build each other up."
1 Thess. 1:11

Wendy, the Woman

*J*t was in September of 2003, that the couple's search for answers led them to UTSW Medical Center where the thorough diagnostic testing and subsequent results left them feeling "relieved!"

"Now we had a name for it," said Peggy. "We felt hope because Jerry was not diagnosed with the fast moving ALS types. We could have hope for a cure while he is still alive," she added.

And, that's when Wendy Davidson, physical therapist, enters this love story.

With an actual diagnosis in hand, Jerry was once again sent off to get help to stave off his declining condition. This visit was destined to change his whole outlook on living and dying.

"There in the pool was Wendy!" said Jerry with glee.

She was the same physical therapist he had seen seven years before. Back then, she was age 21 and newly graduated from college. At that time she had refused to give Jerry therapy treatments because the prescribing doctor had not given her a diagnosis.

"She had said she didn't want to hurt me," Jerry recalled. He said, at that time he was so depressed, he wanted to "just quit" and let the disease take him.

While Wendy did not recognize Jerry, from that previous encounter, he had not forgotten her. She was the one who had given him hope with encouraging words.

This time, Wendy had a diagnosis from UTSW neurologists and she set to work to help build up strength in his withering extremities so he could resist the fearsome disease.

With Wendy he began to see reasons to live.

"It didn't matter what other people thought; I was being treated differently by her. How many people do you know who can motivate you just by talking to you?" he asked rhetorically.

He believed this woman saw him as a real person . . . not just an ailment.

She would say, "See you next time. Don't forget to keep your head up. Do your home exercises. She was uplifting to me and to a lot of other people," said Jerry.

"What I heard from Wendy was that I am worthy. I was someone who mattered," he said incredulously. Up to that point, the disease had been whittling away at Jerry's self-image. Sure, Peggy always was his cheerleader, striving to build his ego, but she was his wife. That was expected. Wendy was a person who didn't know him.

"Here I am disabled, not able to do things and yet, for someone like Wendy, that was not a problem!"

He felt seen.

He felt accepted, despite his infirmities.

"I'd never heard anyone else tell me that they would never give up on me," said Jerry.

For a few years, with water therapy, Jerry was able to maintain balance and use his legs enough to shuffle a few steps. He looked like a penguin, his arms dangling at his sides, as unaided he would venture a short distance buoyed by the water.

"We had some interesting times," Jerry chuckled as he recalled to his interviewer the days of working in a therapy pool.

I accompanied the couple to some of those therapy sessions. Peggy would be at the pool watching while Jerry was in physical therapy three times a week. She would sit there and crochet while keeping an eagle eye on her husband.

One time, walking unaided, Jerry tumbled over, face down into the water.

In an instant, even before Peggy shot up to shout for help, the therapist, at the other end of the pool with another client, dove to the rescue.

"Almost before my face hit with a huge splash, Wendy was there bringing me up out of the water!" Jerry said.

He doubted if Peggy had even missed a stitch on her sewing.

"We had complete trust in Wendy," he said. Peggy, who was listening at his side, nodded agreement.

Sadly, Jerry was obliged to stop the pool therapy routine because he no longer showed even the tiniest bit of improvement. He no longer was a candidate for physical therapy.

Over several years, Peggy had driven thousands of miles transporting her husband to water therapy. Wendy had changed jobs often and sometimes her new employer was opposed to her treating Jerry. They saw him as a hopeless case. Then, Jerry would temporarily seek another physical therapist but he would hound Wendy until she was able from some other therapy clinic to take him back.

Wendy and others treated him for as long as they could. Insurance rules edict that when the patient no longer shows improvement, treatments must stop.

Finally, Wendy could no longer justify treatments for her persistent, long time patient. Jerry had become so obsessed with the idea that she could keep him going that Wendy finally had to completely remove herself from any contact with the Weygandts.

I met with Wendy just before the water therapy came to a halt. She talked about all she had learned from exploring therapy with Jerry and how to care for others with the deadly disease amyotrophic lateral sclerosis. She now travels to professional meetings around the country to report her findings to other physical therapists.

The physical therapist told me she did not see that she "gave up" on this dying man. She maintains she did what she could for as long as she could. Rather, she sees that because of Jerry she has developed life giving skills to extend the days of others who are suffering from this terminal illness.

Jerry and Peggy truly believe his days have been extended because of the special attention and treatment received in water therapy. It made it possible for them to continue association and friendships on monthly recreation vehicle gatherings with their RV club, the Red Rovers as you will see in the next chapter.

"A friend loves at all times."
Proverbs 11:11

Red River Rovers

People who enjoy recreational vehicle trips understand why the Weygandts held onto membership in the Red River Rovers RV Club long after they moved into their house in Plano.

Peggy never felt uneasy about doing what some might see as "man's work" that goes with ownership of a big rig. She loved the RV lifestyle and so did Jerry. She did all the driving of their 38 foot rig and handled all the set up and takedown and other maintenance work that goes along with owning a motor home. She also carried full responsibility for her immobile husband's personal needs.

She saw it as a way for them to continue to feel they were just like any other ordinary couple. Peggy said it was worth the effort to keep going and enjoy the fellowship of RV friends.

Even after it became impossible for them to participate in the motor home club lifestyle they held on to Red River Rovers friends from southern Oklahoma and central north Texas, who take a once a month caravan trip to scenic places.

When travel in their Dutch Star was no longer an option, the couple stayed in a nearby hotel to join friends for the 2009 Annual Fall Rally of the Red River Rovers at the Choctaw Casino on the Texas and Oklahoma border.

They knew it was their "last hurrah" with the RV gang. My husband and I also went to this club gathering to observe and meet the Weygandt's friends.

There were eight guys circled around Jerry's wheelchair laughing and talking in the huge multi-purpose room reserved for the club.

Outside, on the patio, sitting at tables topped with open umbrellas, Peggy sat with a group of women working on a craft project. They were chatting and laughing as hands busily twisted orange and black yarn onto wire coat hangers.

The Weygandts were in their glory. This is what they loved to do for so many years and that weekend would be their "goodbye."

Peggy could no longer handle lifting and guiding Jerry into or out of their rig. He could not assist. The three steps up were too steep and unsafe to maneuver even for the men who had helped in past times.

"I'm the youngest guy in our club, age 55, and it's too much for me," said Ron Hall, a jolly man with thinning hair as he had plunked himself down on a leather sofa to talk about his friends.

Hall, from Duncan, OK, said he once was the "on call guy" for late night assistance getting Jerry into the Weygandts' motor coach after the bonfires and the jokes had died down and it was time for the buddies to break up for the night.

"Jerry is able to tell stories with the best of us—and over and over again just like the rest of us," Hall chuckled.

He was proud of the special bond of friendship the two men shared because of "a wealth of computer knowledge."

"Jerry is a very intelligent, widely read gentleman," said Hall, "if he'd been paid for all his advice, he'd be rich!"

Hall's voice saddened as he recalled the time Jerry was presenting a program to the club using slides. He was unable to lift the slides onto the viewgraph machine.

"Peggy quietly slipped over and asked if I would do it for him."

Hall and his cheery wife, Carol, both say the Weygandts have an "exceptional marriage."

"There's strength of character in both of them that impels them to push on. I've known other marriages where hardship tears people apart. Not Jerry and Peggy! It draws them closer than most marriages I have seen and they have a better sense of humor between each other,"

Back in the dining hall where members gathered for dinner, the Weygandts sat next to Norma and Ron Hamel from Wichita Falls, TX.

They enjoyed light-hearted banter back and forth like friends who have known and cared for each other for many years. Once again, Peggy was feeding Jerry and herself.

He bites.

She bites.

But none of this interrupts the lively conversation going on amongst the several couples at the far end of the long table.

Earlier in the afternoon, Norma had slipped away from the craft group to talk to this writer about her dear friend, Peggy.

"She comes across as strong!"

"She is very strong!"

Norma said this with her brown eyes flashing fire.

Then, just as she had emphasized Peggy's strength of character, the friend's voice quavered and tears filled her eyes, as she talked about her tender side.

"Peggy can also break down and cry."

The friend, who is pint-sized like Peggy, sounded especially concerned for her friend's welfare as a caregiver.

"Jerry is a practical joker. He's very upbeat all the time. But sometimes it's not so funny," confided Norma.

She went on to describe how early in their friendship Jerry teasingly asked Norma to bring him a donut because his wife wouldn't do it for him.

"I'll go get you one," Norma said she offered.

Then she had turned to Peggy and jokingly chided her saying, "Why won't you go get this *poor man* a donut?"

Norma described how tears started to trickle down Peggy's cheeks and then she heard her say in barely a whisper, "Jerry's a diabetic. He's not to have a donut."

Norma winced as she told of feeling sad and ashamed for having teased Peggy.

"But it wasn't fair of Jerry to set me up that way," she added shaking her head.

The longtime RV friends said they were sad to think that the Weygandts would not be participating in future rallies.

"This (RV club) has been a lifeline for Peggy," Norma said.

". . . there is a friend that sticks
closer than a brother."
Proverbs 18:24

Wendy, the Dog

She was an adorable little English Golden Labrador Retriever puppy when she entered Jerry and Peggy's world early in 2008 under the urging of their son and daughter-in-law, Lee and Maureen Bowman.

Some thought the frisky little dog was just like the cute puppy in a name brand dog food commercial on television.

Peggy is prone to drop everything to accommodate her husband's wishes. The Bowman's saw that a trained assist dog would be good for Jerry and also might give her a little uninterrupted break to load a dishwasher, straighten up the kitchen and do other household chores.

They saw that Jerry was not going to sit back and give up his passionate interest and involvement in his church, civic or ALS assistance affairs. His step-son and daughter-in-law said they admired his determination to be seen, heard and respected even though he was helplessly strapped into a wheelchair.

"We knew a woman who trained assist dogs and felt it would be good for Jerry to have one. The dog has a good calming influence on them both," explained Maureen privately.

The little golden haired puppy was instantly named "Wendy" because Jerry saw the dog would be a bright and golden star in his and Peggy's lives just like an especially appreciated physical therapist, named Wendy, was at that time.

The puppy was about nine weeks old when she was placed with the couple. When Wendy, the dog, is on duty she wears a pink vest that tells the dog she is to be alert to commands to serve her master's special needs.

In the beginning, that was to include training the dog to use her nose to nudge the toggle on the arm of the old wheelchair to propel Jerry forward. The dog would also use her paw to turn light switches off or on or open the front door lever.

Sadly, Jerry's condition worsened so that he needed a high tech wheelchair with multiple electronic gadgets to do most of what the dog was to do.

However, that has not held Wendy the dog back from becoming the faithful friend and "calming influence" at Jerry's side wherever he went including church, restaurants and shopping malls.

G-O-D and D-O-G

The more deeply I, Beverly, delved into my Spiritual Direction course work, the more I saw the Weygandts as examples of holding to faith in adversity. They witness not with sermonizing words, but with the way they live their lives. Like Job in the Old Testament, they tenaciously hold to faith in a loving God.

One day, after class, I stopped by the Weygandts house on my way home. Our class had just had a discussion on how do we see God. Is God a thundering tyrant from on high? Is God a gentle shepherd leading his sheep? We get our first impressions of God from childhood experiences.

How does Jerry see God? I wondered.

He was in a relaxed mood, happy to see his surprise visitor, so I broached the subject on that Friday call.

"What does God look like to you?" I asked.

"Oh," he said, "God loves me just as I am and so does my dog Wendy!"

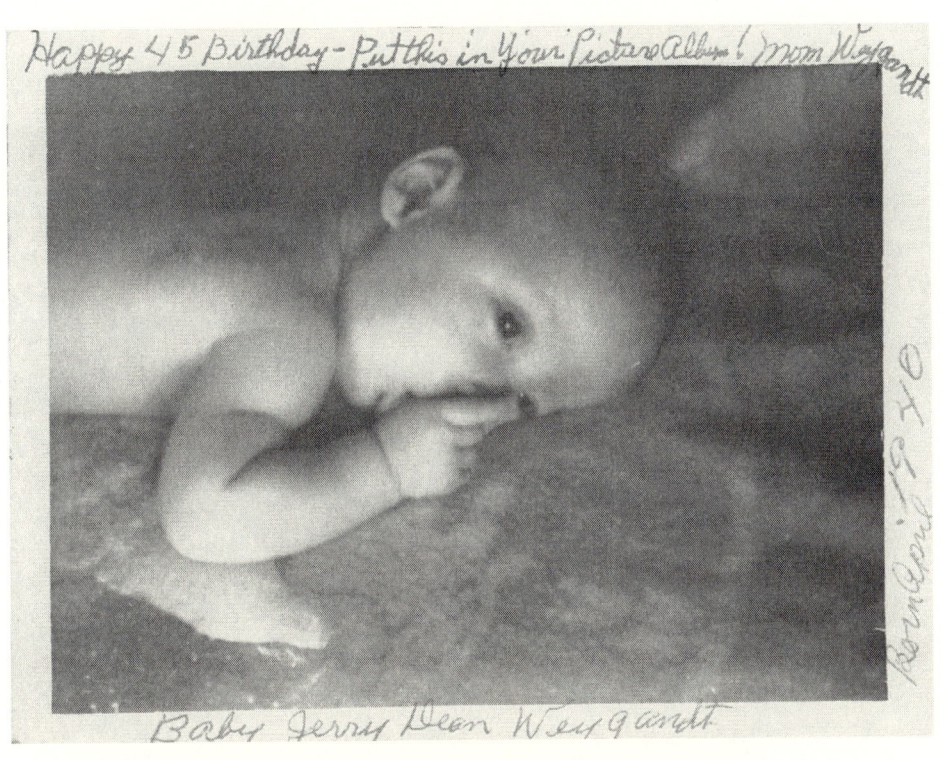

Jerry Weygandt baby picture.

Jerry Weygandt high school picture 1958.

Newlyweds, Jerry and Peggy, center, pose with their blended family of six sons and her Mother, Mabel Dravenstatt.

Jerry rests against rock on Grand Canyon hike.

Jerry and Peggy Weygandt photo taken in 1985.

Jerry posed for a church directory picture in 2002.

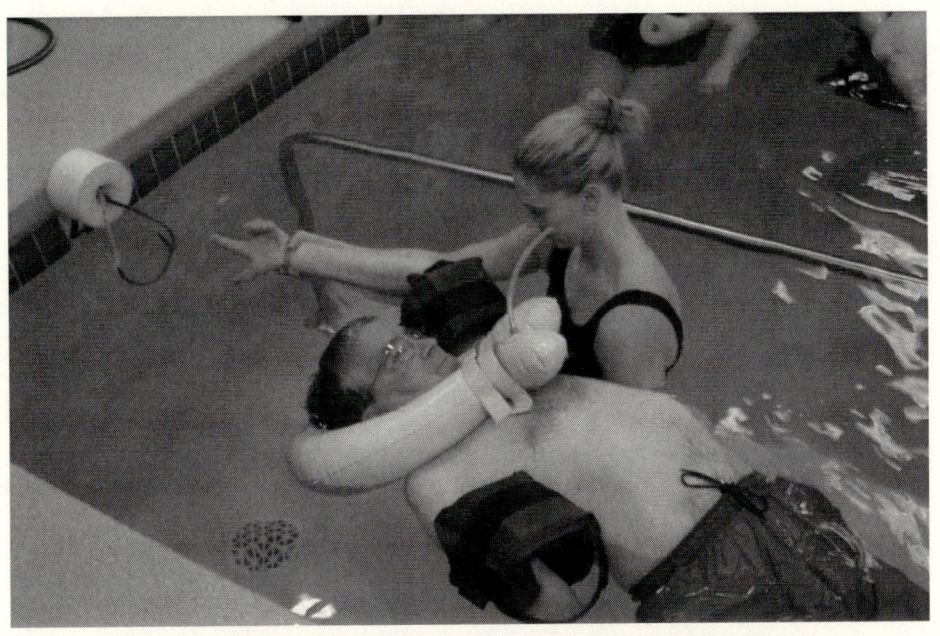

Wendy, the physical therapist, does water therapy with Jerry in 2006 to help him stave off loss of muscle strength.

Jerry and Peggy Weygandt with friends on a 2006 ALS Walk to raise funds for research.

Jerry gets acquainted with his six weeks old puppy named Wendy.

Peggy and Jerry enjoy celebrating their wedding anniversary with
a special dinner party at Baileys on December 19, 2009.

Wendy, the dog, keeps sentry with his dying master in November 2011.

". . . The kingdom of God is within you."
Luke 17:21

In the King's Service

"Jerry would not be able to sit in his chair like a king if it weren't for Peggy!"

That comment came from a church lady to mutual friends at the close of the Harmony Sunday School class. It was early summer 2008, and folks were strolling out from the FUMC Upper Room Chapel to the elevator.

Barbara Urban speaks her mind. She is also one with a generous heart and can be counted on to volunteer help when needed.

Mrs. Urban answered the call for help when the Weygandts returned home from a trip to see family in Ohio. Peggy was laid up with a dislocated shoulder, an injury she received in a fall in a dimly lit hospital parking lot where they had gone to visit a relative. Back in Plano, Peggy reported that after that accident, she "just wanted to go home!"

Peggy said she didn't remember how she managed to care for her totally dependent passenger or drive the one thousand plus miles home but somehow she made it despite being heavily sedated on pain pills.

Back home, word spread that the Weygandts needed help. That's when the church lady experienced what caregiver Peggy faced daily in routine care for Jerry.

"You have no idea what responsibility lies on that little woman's shoulders until you offer to give some help," Mrs. Urban huffed to me at the close of Sunday morning class.

She went on to describe how her intention had been only to bring dinner and leave but upon arrival, she saw it would be best to stay and feed Jerry and help straighten up the house a bit.

Mrs. Urban described how she had observed Peggy, arm in a sling, struggling as best she could to feed Jerry.

"I just don't know how she does it," she told me later.

"All I did was prepare a meal, feed Jerry, and clean up the kitchen. Peggy has all her housework *plus* doing everything for Jerry from dressing him to combing his hair, brushing his teeth, cooking his meals, feeding him and lifting him into and out of his wheelchair. All the things a person with useful arms and legs can do for oneself, Peggy does for Jerry," she raved.

"And, she smiles and does it so lovingly!"

When the church lady's remarks were repeated later to Peggy she sighed and smiled.

"I don't see what I do for Jerry as anything so unusual. You do what you have to do because you love that person and you want life to be the best it can be for them. If it were reversed, I know Jerry would do it for me."

Then, after a long, reflective pause, she added, "And God sends angels like church friends to assist when we need extra help."

Peggy doesn't consider herself to be a "martyr."

She knows how to take care of herself and she does it as best she can. She is intentional about making sure she holds faithful to some things just for herself. She enjoys the luxury of regularly having her fingenails done and often goes so far as to have fancy artwork on two or more of them.

"It's something I like to do for me," she said, flashing brightly painted pink nails with tiny rosebuds painted on her little fingers.

". . . the cheerful heart has a continual feast."
Proverbs 15:15

The Entourage

Over time, while Jerry was still able, the couple regularly visited numerous restaurants in the neighborhoods of their home and church. They enjoyed being out to see the construction boom taking place, especially in Collin County, Texas, one of the fastest growing areas in the nation.

They frequently made return visits to places like Napoli's, an Italian restaurant in an Allen strip mall with a Wal-Mart neighborhood grocery on one end and the little eatery on the other. At this place when they saw Jerry coming, the waiter would alert the cook and often he would have Jerry's order started before the handicapped man got through the door.

The Weygandts favored exploring places opening up in the fast growing commercial area of the Villages of Allen and Fairview, a short distance north of Plano and Dallas off Highway 75. The two would stake out a new restaurant during the week and then suggest it for the group on Sunday.

Jerry liked to go out riding in the van. He is keenly aware of The American Disability Act, laws favoring the handicapped, and so if he spotted a vehicle illegally parked in a handicapped space, or a telephone pole blocking wheelchair passage on a sidewalk, a missing sidewalk ramp or any barrier to easy access for the disabled he would take measures to make things right. That often meant dispatching Peggy to speak to the driver of an illegally parked vehicle, or an authority or to send a message to the City of Plano or City of Allen stating his concerns. And those concerns usually got swift action for correction of these complaints. He had even attended Plano City Council meetings to personally speak his mind.

One typical Sunday at a newly opened place on in Allen, the manager graciously welcomed our party of eight and led us to a long table hastily set for the group.

The restaurant was noisy and packed with an overflow crowd cramming the entry and spilling out the door onto the sidewalk. The sea of humanity parted. Jerry, as if he were making a regal entry, rolled through the crowd with Wendy, the golden lab assist dog at his side. Peggy led the way. The elderly, youth, parents, some holding infants, others tending hungry, cranky, rambunctious, children, all stepped aside.

We, in the Weygandt party, tagged along behind as if we were part of a royal's entourage.

Later, the manager dropped by our table to ask if we were satisfied with the service.

"Yes," we heartily replied.

I asked the spiky, red haired host if anyone ever complained about the appearance of preferential treatment for the handicapped man and his friends.

"Noooooo," the cheery young manager had said,

"What I do notice is that children ask to pet the dog and then the adults get drawn in by the kids. Children will crawl under the table to get to the dog," he said.

And, as the manager departed, that's just what happened.

A little girl approached.

"May I pet your dog?" she shyly asked.

Then with a smile from Jerry she scrambled under the table and began to pat Wendy, the dog. Curious children do not hesitate to ask questions and Peggy patiently answered all the little girl's inquiries. She told the wide eyed child that assist dogs are permitted in restaurants and all public places, and "even church."

"So then, whenever we have an opportunity, let us work for the good of all, and especially for those in the family of faith."
Galatians 6:10

Harmony Friends

One Valentine's Day, Jerry and Peggy home delivered a single long stemmed American Beauty rose to each one of a dozen or so women who helped with food and other assistance during a time when Peggy had been laid up with illness.

It was their way to say thank you.

Church friends are usually the first to respond to the Weygandts when they need help. They are folks from a senior's class named Harmony after the Bible verse in Romans 12:16 *"Let us live in harmony with one another."*

"We have been so blessed," Peggy gushed to the friend opening her door to receive a red rose. The Weygandts are grateful for the outpouring of love and attention they receive from faithful friends that continues to this day.

Harmony friend Virginia Haley and her husband Chuck, both in their eighties, are generous responders to needs of their elderly classmates. Making home and hospital visits, delivering meals, actively supporting XYZ (Extra Years of Zest) monthly luncheons and Friday Night Games, checkers, cards, dominos, in the church parlor, that were often also attended by the Weygandts.

Chuck has been known to stay through the night at Jerry's bedside in the hospital when Peggy just could not be there.

"Theirs is an amazing love story," is how Mrs. Haley described her friends to me one morning on our way out of Sunday class.

One Smooth, Continuous Motion

Back in 2008, Peggy was still transporting herself and Jerry in a worn down tan Chevrolet Trailblazer van with a lift on the back to carry Jerry's old wheelchair. It was up to her to position the chair just right beside the passenger door to help him get inside the van. Then she would push the empty chair around back and secure it on the lift before driving off. Rainy days and cold and windy weather made this all the more difficult.

Peggy might be small but she is strong! She was able in one continuous motion to swiftly lift, turn and smoothly move her husband's limp body into an upright position for entering the old van. He would briefly steady himself and she would help him scoot up onto the front seat.

But, the process was strenuous and Peggy constantly feared she would drop him.

They had taken a fast trip to a hospital with Jerry bleeding profusely from a gash on his forehead when she had lost her grip and he tumbled on a sidewalk. Peggy hoped to find an affordable used vehicle that would have a side slider door and entry ramp so Jerry could stay in his chair while being transported.

The guys up the road in Plano Fire Station Six had given her a direct line to call because of the frequency with which they were needed to come and pick Jerry up off the bedroom floor when she struggled to get him into or out of bed.

At that time, Jerry was still able to participate in a group of retired men who gather every Wednesday morning for coffee and conversation. Afterward, the guys would continue their discussion by going out for lunch.

Peggy knew it was important for Jerry to have this social time with male friends for as long as he was able. She needed a break to be with her women friends. So Wednesdays, while he was with the group, 'Men Talking,' she would toss the van keys to one of two men friends who would take turns for "Jerry Duty." Then Peggy would be picked up at the church to go to lunch with her women friends.

Peggy still treasures this time when she is able to get away.

"For one meal a week I did not have to feed Jerry. I could just be me enjoying my friends."

But, it was not easy for her to trust her husband in any other person's care.

It is no wonder that Peggy was adamant about her instructions to special friend Duane Lingenfelter when she handed him the van keys. She wanted to be certain he could handle the lift and turn and lift again process to get Jerry out of his wheelchair and safely into the van.

Oooooooops!!!

Duane is a man with a hearty laugh that goes with his barrel chested physique,

He enjoys telling a good story including the one about how he, "sort of dropped Jerry."

"I had him up and standing out of his wheelchair and leaning against me," said Duane. This was several years ago at the end of a Men Talking meeting at the church.

Duane described how he was "about to get Jerry turned to hoist him onto the van seat when the helpless handicapped man started slowly slipping down out of his grasp.

Duane said he tried to hold on to Jerry but the two men started laughing so hard it just wasn't working.

"I tried to stop his slide with my knee. That wasn't such a good idea. And, we laughed all the more!"

Throwing his head back with a laugh, the storyteller said, "Here we were, two grown men in a church parking lot and we appeared to be hugging and hysterically laughing. We must have been a sight to anyone watching."

Duane remembers that the two made a pact not to tell Peggy because they didn't want to upset her.

"Then, the first thing we did when we saw her was . . . tell her!" said Duane with another booming laugh.

One good turn . . .

Bob Cochran was a much loved and admired member of the Harmony Sunday School Class, the Men Talking group and the Friday ROMEOS (Retired Old Men Eating Out).

He was a gentleman. He was a man with a huge compassionate heart. He had a dry sense of humor and enjoyed engaging people in conversation.

Often, at Sunday brunch, Bob, a tall, distinguished, but fragile looking elderly man would chat with a waiter or waitress to learn about their lives. He readily offered encouraging words. When Bob became aware of a need, he would sometimes anonymously follow up with a monetary gift to offer help.

The former Chief Financial Officer for Chrysler Financial Credit Company had experienced numerous heartaches within a short span of time in his declining years. It started with the tragic death of a daughter from cancer, and then lingering illness and death of his beloved wife, Sally. Subsequently, Bob went on to quietly deal with his own grief and serious health problems while offering love and care to an ailing brother and sister-in-law in Tennessee until these family members also died. It seemed the more personal pain Bob faced, the more generous he became to others.

He was a sure visitor to anyone who was hospitalized or in a nursing home.

He was especially fond of Peggy and Jerry Weygandt. He admired Peggy for her spunk and courage in caring for her husband. She resembled his Sally in size and spirit. So when Bob's wife died, he generously gave some of Sally's clothing to Peggy. Mr. Cochran saw the couple was struggling financially. It had been many years since Peggy had bought any new clothing for herself.

The spring day she showed up in a delicate mint green pant suit, I observed the pleasure on Bob's face as he quietly watched Peggy turn this way and that to model her new outfit.

"I wish her well," he said.

"What good is it my brothers and sisters
if you say you have faith but have no deeds?"
James 2:14

Faith and Deeds

Wherever they went . . . and from previous chapters you know that was lots of places . . . their presence would speak volumes about their faith.

Jerry is not the kind of guy to waste time worrying over what he could or could not do. He just forged ahead.

He was on a mission.

"I say, cure yourself of the affliction of caring how you look to others. You should only concern yourself with the impression that God may have of you," he said to his interviewer.

Jerry's hope was that when people saw a paralyzed man in a wheelchair in public places participating in a variety of events they would see just another guy out and about.

It has only been since 2011 that Jerry has had to halt venturing out.

He urges others with ALS to not give up early (in their diagnosis) and just sit around waiting to die.

DART Adventure

Several years ago, Jerry, in his wheelchair, and Peggy braved a night out taking the DART train some 50 miles from Plano to Fort Worth for a Gaither Brothers' Concert.

"The concert got out late at night and we were the only people waiting for the DART (Dallas Area Rapid Transit). It was dark. It was after one o'clock in the morning before we got back home," said Peggy.

When Peggy relayed the adventure to Harmony classmates the next morning, I overheard several of their senior citizen friends expressed amazement.

Jerry just smiled.

He told the group, "I'm not going to let this illness keep me from living life."

The Voice of God

With hundreds of thousands of people living in the Dallas—Fort Worth metroplex what are the chances that the Weygandts would connect miles away from home with an acquaintance of a friend of theirs?

They did.

I, Beverly, began to suspect that my friend Juanita Rischard, a counselor in private practice, was talking about the Weygandts when she raved about an unusual experience she had at her orthopedic surgeon's office.

"I heard the voice of God!" she had excitedly revealed

Juanita is no nut case. She is a rock solid, sane woman with two master's degrees, one in science education and another in counseling.

Juanita said she had been to her orthopedic surgeon's office for follow up after an operation that had left her homebound in a wheelchair with her right foot and leg in a cast for many weeks. The doctor had just removed a big, heavy cast and replaced it with a lighter one that she would wear for another six weeks. After that she would be back on her feet using crutches and then a cane.

I knew about Juanita's situation because she and I are both spiritual directors and often attend continuing education seminars together. It was while transporting my friend Juanita and her wheelchair to a seminar that she told me about her experience with "God."

Juanita said that when she re-entered the doctor's waiting room after her visit to the specialist she had gleefully announced to all that she would only have to put up with her cast for another six weeks.

That's when she heard "God's voice."

Juanita described how a low basso, resonant, authoritative man's voice from behind her said, "I wish I only had six weeks in this chair."

When Juanita whirled around to see who was speaking, she saw a man in a wheelchair and a smiling woman standing, not much taller than the man in sitting in the chair, at his side.

Juanita said in that moment she felt ashamed for complaining about her temporary handicap and determined in the future she would look for ways to be grateful.

Later, I relayed Juanita's story to the Weygandts, and they readily admitted they were the couple she was talking about. They had been in the doctor's office for Peggy's dislocated left shoulder mentioned in a previous chapter about a trip to Ohio.

Jerry was grinning when he told me, "I'm pleased to have influenced her to look at situations in a different way. She will remember it the next time she is around someone in a wheelchair."

ALS SUPPORT GROUPS

Jerry's been physically making statements for wheelchair bound people for many years by faithfully attending ALS Support Group monthly meetings in a Plano church sponsored by the ALS Association of North Texas.

Several times a year, he and Peggy also attended a support group meeting at the Bachman Lake facility some 30 miles south of Dallas sponsored by the ALS division of Muscular Dystrophy Association.

It is only since 2010 that the couple quit attending these meetings. Peggy would muster up the energy to get her husband to these evening sessions because he said it was important to him to be present.

"I see myself as an encourager for others, especially those who are newly diagnosed with ALS and feeling so scared," was his way of explaining why it was so necessary to attend even on those nights when it took extra effort to go.

He and Peggy have watched a parade of ALS people come and go as the often fast moving disease takes their lives.

When I attended with the couple I found myself in a large multipurpose room of a church. There were about forty people encircling the perimeter area and about every third or fourth person, sat in a wheelchair. Some were able to sit up and others were in reclining positions.

None were able to raise their hands so I found it ludicrous that the speaker that evening asked for a "raise of hands" for those who had been helped by a certain handicap appliance.

The people accompanying the ALS patients were mostly spouses or other family members and some were likely paid caretakers. All seemed intently interested in anything that would help them deal with this deadly disease.

Jerry and Peggy had pretty much heard it all over the years they'd been attending. He saw attending ALS support meetings as just that, a way to learn more for himself and to offer some seasoned survival tactics. Peggy's purpose was to show other caregivers to not lose heart. She has developed an Advice for Caregivers list (see back pages) which she has presented at panel discussion meetings.

"For some it may be only a matter of months," Jerry told me sadly.

That evening he advised the ALS group, "To be able to live with a diagnosis of ALS, you have to be able to exist one day at a time. If you worry about what is going to happen to you (on another day) you won't be able to live today."

Jerry said he knows his future is already figured out.

"My body is going in a grave."

He said it as a matter of fact.

Then his face took on an even more serious demeanor.

"We are just practicing now. The Bible tells us there are better times ahead. Upon our death, we will no longer have ALS".

Pastors and Friends

S mall children would scurry out of worship services to find Wendy, the service dog and Jerry, her master, as soon as the last hymn was sung on Sunday morning.

For many years, leading up to 2011 when he was no longer able, it was Jerry's practice, at the close of the service, to turn his wheelchair around and follow the pastors up the center aisle of the sanctuary and out the wide doors to the open area beyond.

In this gathering place is a labyrinth. Designed into the marble floor is a huge circular maze that the faithful may, at quiet private times, walk and pray. On Sundays, Jerry would position his wheelchair right in the center of the labyrinth. From this prime spot, he could be seen from all four of the directions leading to the sanctuary.

And, Jerry loved it. He was pleased to be noticed!

He intentionally chose this particular spot and time so that people coming or leaving could not avoid seeing him. It was the time between the morning worship services.

What they saw was a pale, gaunt man, visibly diminishing as the weeks and months wore on. He sat motionless in his chair. His head held rigid in a head rest. His helpless scrawny forearms and long, splayed out ghost white fingers lay helplessly on the white lamb's wool arms of the chair. Yet, there was always a welcoming grin on his face and his huge wide brown eyes would surf the masses of people surging into the area. Some would trot right past. Others would see his welcoming smile, pause to talk, or wave as they passed by.

There were two or three other church members in wheelchairs and over time there became a growing camaraderie among these people. Sometimes one or two would station their chairs near their friend, Jerry.

But, it was the children he seemed to enjoy most as little hands tugged at an able bodied adult and urged, "Come meet my friend and Wendy, his dog."

Jerry saw this routine as a way to fulfill his calling.

He believes with all his heart that God is directing him to be seen and be an advocate for the disabled. So he greets the children with the 'open arms' he cannot use to show them this encounter is a normal experience.

One Sunday, I watched from a short distance, when a tiny girl with blonde curly hair and huge blue eyes toddled determinedly through the maze of grownups. She plopped down, nose-to-nose with the golden lab lying next to the wheelchair. The tot pulled two sticky fingers from her mouth and patted the sandy haired dog.

After a bit, she stood up, and shyly smiled at Jerry.

He returned her grin.

Fingers back in her mouth, she studied the man in the chair and slowly backed away.

There was an expression of perfect contentment on the disabled man's face.

Jerry knew he was exactly where God want him to be!

Pastor Todd Harris

The Rev. Todd Harris, senior pastor of First United Methodist Church of Allen that has a membership of 2,000 and is growing. On the north wall, behind his desk, are floor to ceiling polished wood shelves lined with books and other objects valued by this cheery, 49 year old native Texan.

The pastor greeted me warmly.

I commented on the various crosses arranged on the wall by his door and the plethora of family photos on the credenza standing against that wall. This is a family man who takes pride in his attractive wife and their two young children.

After a bit of casual conversation about the avid fly fisherman's trip to Colorado, we get right to the purpose of our meeting, his impressions of Jerry.

"Jerry is a living witness to Christ's message to his church," said the senior pastor. He had regularly observed Jerry and his assist dog from the minister's Sunday morning hand-shaking station at the sanctuary's center door exit.

The pastor seemed genuinely pleased to speak about this faithful parishioner.

"Without moving a muscle or speaking a word, Jerry's life is a sermon." he said.

"Jerry shows in his weakness his acceptance of God's love and strength. He has told me that he truly believes he is serving God by making the most of his life just as it is in the wheelchair. He wants to encourage others (who are handicapped) to see that they can still serve God and live purpose filled lives."

The energetic pastor with a wry humor said he didn't mind having a dog in church. The minister said he felt certain Wendy, the dog, paid close attention to his sermons.

"On Sundays when we go over time, such as for baptisms or receiving new members, Wendy will let me know it's time to go by a muffled signal, not really a bark, but just a little ruff sound," said the smiling Pastor Todd.

"Folks just seem to delight in Wendy. She never disturbs the service. My guess is most people don't even realize there's a dog in church unless they see her entering or leaving the sanctuary," he added.

Blessing Abound

The Rev. June Franck was usually the one to serve Holy Communion to the Weygandts. She would take the elements to the place where the couple was seated. As pastoral care minister, the Rev. Franck is well acquainted with the Weygandts. She is the one they call first when faced with a crisis.

The first Sunday that Wendy the dog, attended church, Pastor June, as she is lovingly called, was momentarily shocked to see Peggy share her piece of Holy Communion bread, given to be the body of Christ, with the dog!

The petite minister, who annually presides at the Blessing of the Animals, quickly recovered. After all, if she can pray over and touch snakes and other reptilian pets, what is there to worry about with a dog taking the sacraments?

The pastor said she realizes, "The dog, Wendy, is a gift from God to bless Jerry's and Peggy's remarkable spiritual journey."

"Who am I to question what God can do through the body of Christ?" she said. Since that incident, this pastor always carries three pieces of bread to serve Holy Communion to the Weygandts. Since the close of 2010 the pastor has served the Eucharist to Jerry at his home where he is confined to a hospital bed. A Hospice nurse now attends Jerry on Sunday mornings so that Peggy can attend church and continue to join her friends for lunch.

The pretty minister with the sparkling smile told her interviewer that she sees the ailing Jerry as the epitome of 1 John 4:18.

"Perfect love drives out fear," she explained in her lovely, soft voice that reminds one of birds singing.

Revelation's Revelation

"I miss Jerry's input," said David Frank when I visited with him to ask about the former regular Harmony Class member who would park his wheelchair in the front row in the Upper Room Chapel for class.

Jerry was not able to turn pages in a Bible but he was a student of daily scripture reading and study on the internet for as long as he could sit in his wheelchair up to his specially designed computer. Teacher Franck, who is married to the Rev. Franck, says he used to urge Jerry to help "stir the pot" to build class discussions.

Revelations, the last book in the New Testament is not a popular choice for Bible study. This book deals with end times and uses hard to decipher symbolism. Maybe, senior citizens and Jerry in particular, have greater interest because death is not so far away for them.

At any rate, one time when David Franck, known for his scholarly research, was suddenly unavailable to teach the class, Jerry whipped his wheelchair around to face the class and proceeded to report from memory all he had read and learned from the internet about The Book of Revelations.

"My grace is sufficient for you, for my power
is made perfect in weakness."
2 Cor. 12:9

Amazing Grace

It was a Sunday morning in November 2009.
The sanctuary of First United Methodist Church of Allen
was filled with people of all ages, including visitors in the area for the
Thanksgiving holiday.

Jerry saw this as the perfect time to surprise the congregation by joining
the choir and other musicians in a special presentation of the famous John
Newton hymn, *"Amazing Grace."*

Jerry had been reminiscing about the days when he sang with the
church praise team in Indiana. This led him to picture himself singing this
favorite hymn in church in Allen. And, he speculated, why shouldn't or
couldn't a paralyzed man in a wheelchair sing a solo in church?

"I feel such gratitude. I hold such fondness for the people in our church.
I wanted them to see God's amazing grace is for all of us."

Jerry believes his illness has influenced how he and Peggy see amazing
grace in their lives. He cites the move to Indiana, finding the job at New
Hope United Methodist Church and how that church family rallied around
them at the start of their deepening awareness of God's presence in their
lives.

"Everything centered on the church," Jerry once told me, speculating
that he and Peggy were "on the road to get found."

On that Thanksgiving Sunday, Jerry rolled up the center aisle, turned
to face the congregation, and was ready to sing.

Standing proudly beside her grandfather was Lana Bowman, a high school student. When Jerry began to sing, the girl raised her arms and gracefully signed the words.

The Rev. Brian McPherson directed the musicians. The organist played that wonderful old hymn with the traditional American melody in an arrangement by Chris Tomlin and Louie Griglio.

"Amazing grace how sweet the sound
That saved a wretch like me!
I once was lost but now am found
Was blind but now I see"

His voice wavered a little and he was a tad off key but that just made it all the more touching to the rapt, listening congregation. The choir joined in and the music swelled. People dabbed tears from their eyes as the music soared and carried on to Jerry's next solo part. This time, instead of singing, his strong, bass voice spoke the words to a new verse titled *"My Chains are Gone."*

"My chains are gone,
I've been set free.
My God, my Savior,
Has ransomed me.

And like a flood
His mercy reigns,
Unending love,
Amazing grace."

Peggy says she held her breath as the song continued. It was Jerry's moment and she proudly sat in their regular place on the center aisle with Wendy the dog at her feet. She felt thrilled to see her husband perform with the choir. She knew how much this meant to him.

"The earth shall soon
Dissolve like snow.
The sun forbear to shine.
But God who called me here below,
Will be forever mine."

Peggy had her back to most of the congregation. As the anthem came to an end, she heard rustling behind her.

People began to clap.

The clapping continued and got louder.

Peggy turned and saw all were standing in an ovation expressing appreciation to Jerry and the choir.

"That's when I lost it," Peggy later reported, tears once again welling up in her eyes.

"I was so touched by all the love and support given to Jerry," she said.

Unseen Visitor

Wendy, the physical therapist, had sat quietly in the back of the church on the Sunday when Jerry sang *"Amazing Grace."*

"It was Jerry's moment. I was just thrilled to be here to hear him sing and to know what an inspiration he is to others," she told the woman who had spotted her in the back row and had caught up to Wendy as she was quickly leaving the church.

"Ask, and it will be given to you; search and you will find; knock,
and the door will be opened for you.
Matthew 7:7

The Windfall

Frugal!
That best describes how Jerry and Peggy were with their money.

Frugality is the only lifestyle either one of them had ever known. It was the way of life from their growing up years as small town and farm kids in Ohio.

It didn't change while they raised six sons. They pulled the money belt tight.

Even after the boys had all left home and it was just the two of them running their own electrical business with computer work and sales on the side, they wouldn't have described themselves as financially well off.

With Jerry's illness there were times when the couple found themselves at the end of the money before the end of the month. Their expenses grew as Jerry became more and more helpless. Sometimes Peggy would forgo Wednesday lunch dates because she didn't have the money.

That is why together they worked hard covering every angle to be approved for a disability rating from the United States Veterans Administration. It would make a huge difference in how they could afford to handle Jerry's care.

"We didn't think anything would likely come of it but we kept at it!" Peggy described.

The people at ALS support group meetings had encouraged the couple to make inquiries about a new law benefiting all who had served in the military and had subsequently been diagnosed with Amyotrophic Lateral Sclerosis. Jerry had joined the Army at age 17 and served six months active duty at Fort Jackson, S. C. He was in the active Army Reserves for another four years and then inactive four more years. It was just before the Vietnam War.

Tenacious might be too mild a word to describe the campaign the couple embarked upon to see if Jerry would qualify for Veteran's Administration benefits. Peggy wrote letters. She made endless phone calls. They made personal visits all up and down the line hounding anyone they thought could help; from Collin County's Senator Sam Johnson to Texas State Senator Kay Bailey Hutchinson to Governor Rick Perry.

Jerry explained that years and years ago his military records had been burned in a fire at the U.S. Army Records storage facility in St. Louis, Mo. There also were mix-ups with both his and Peggy's Social Security numbers and the tangled mess just went on and on.

"How many times do you hear 'No' before you just give up?" Jerry had wondered. Yet, he and Peggy refused to take 'No' for an answer.

Tenacity paid off!

Much to their amazement, a phone call one August morning in 2009 from the United States Veterans Administration regional office in Waco, Texas changed everything.

It was the windfall they had been praying for!

"It was a miracle!" said Peggy

The VA man said he needed to verify Social Security numbers and their bank account number because he was going to be depositing "a rather large amount of money and he wouldn't want it to go to the wrong account."

The VA quest had been a hot topic at lunch for months, wondering if the money would ever be granted, so when Peggy told her women friends the good news she was dancing up and down with glee.

Drawing in a deep breath, she said she had asked the man what he meant by "rather large amount?"

He informed her that Jerry had been declared 100 percent disabled and qualified for VA disability pension and that the pension was retroactive to September of 2008.

Indeed, it was a big chunk of money! It was several thousands of dollars.

The Weygandts are not comfortable giving out the pension's exact amount, but suffice to say, the disability grants available were sufficient to make health and home improvements to better care for Jerry and give Peggy some relief. They receive a monthly pension for as long as Jerry lives and Peggy will get widow's benefits after her husband dies.

Answered Prayers

Here's a partial list of how the US Veterans Administration Grant has made life better for Jerry and Peggy Weygandt:

- They have a brand new white 2010 Chrysler Town & Country van, designed to accommodate a handicapped person. It has a ramp so Jerry just drives his wheelchair up and into the van. Peggy then locks it into place and away they go.
- Jerry has a state of the art wheelchair that responds to the slightest touch of his chin to move forward and or back. It also is wired to voice respond to open the front door or answer the phone.
- The master bedroom has a special lift to aid in getting the paralyzed man into or out of his new adjustable hospital bed. (*Peggy's new single bed fits right next to Jerry's bed so happily, they still feel like they are sleeping side-by-side.*)
- There is another lift apparatus to transport Jerry from the bed or wheelchair into the bathroom. (*Peggy used to have to use all her physical strength to get Jerry into the bathroom and onto the commode or into and out of their regular bathtub. Now they have a large tiled shower space to accommodate a Likorail apparatus and sling that does the lifting and transporting of Jerry in the bathroom and bedroom. And they have a paid nurse's aide to do the work.*)
- All the doors in the 1,800 square foot house have been widened to accommodate the wheelchair. There is a new front door and two exterior side doors. There are slightly sloping sidewalks to accommodate wheelchair movement. (*They had been putting up with an old front door that was hung wrong so it made entries and exits cumbersome. The ramp was a make-do sheet of plywood.*)
- Hardwood floors have replaced carpets worn threadbare from the wheels on Jerry's old chair. (*Peggy was thrilled with the new look to her home and to the easier access the floors make for Jerry's chair.*)
- The kitchen has been remodeled for easier wheelchair access, removing a center island cupboard. (*Peggy says her kitchen chores get done much more efficiently in this new arrangement.*)
- The front and side yards have been landscaped with a concrete patio that slightly slopes from the kitchen side door to enable Jerry easily to move to the outdoors. (*Peggy said it had been years since Jerry was able to sit outside with her. The First United Methodist*

Church of Allen youth spent a weekend planting shrubs and flowers around the exterior of the house. The FUMCA Facility work group and youth groups have voluntarily worked on keeping flowers planted and the yard looking good.)

- A visiting nurse's aide comes three times a week to attend to Jerry's personal hygiene needs. A physical therapist, until recently would come twice a week to work with him to help stave off the insidious muscle weakness taking over his entire body's strength.

- Since 2011 Hospice has been in charge of Jerry's medical care; sometimes 24/7 for many weeks and then Jerry will rally and Hospice will cut back hours leaving Peggy to handle it alone again except for certain times like Sundays so she can be away to attend church, lunch with friends and do some quick errands before returning home for "Jerry Duty." *(Peggy also qualifies for respite care . . . meaning she can periodically take a long weekend and check into a motel to catch up on lost sleep while Hospice tends full time to Jerry.)*

- The cleaning lady comes weekly to keep the house picked up and in good order. *(This was a task that Peggy would guiltily let slide because she always puts Jerry's needs first.)*

Life has become so much easier!" Peggy joyously described after ticking off the list of home improvements, special equipment and assistance the VA has provided.

Shortly after receiving their good fortune, Jerry offered thoughts about their "windfall" answer to prayers.

"You have to be able to ask and be able to give. The Bible says to ask, seek, find. We are told to care for others. Be an example. I believe Peg and I are able to graciously receive kindnesses and we also continue to find ways to give back. To do what we can to offer kindness and appreciation to others."

And, that's what inspired them to host an open house to show caring folks what their prayers and concern had brought to their friends.

"Offer hospitality to one another . . ."
1 Peter 4:9

Open House

To the Weygandts' delight, 75 people, including their pastors, church friends, recreational vehicle pals, neighbors, firefighters and caregivers, showed up and signed the guest book up for an Open House in August 2010 to view the new changes that the Veterans Administration grant made possible.

"I didn't know so many people cared about us!"

That was how Peggy gleefully described the event a few days later.

"They just kept on coming!"

While his condition was rapidly deteriorating, Jerry was still able to greet guests from his wheelchair at that time.

The Weygandts wanted to show appreciation to all the folks who have expressed care and concern for them.

Some asked for a demonstration of the new ceiling track and lift in the master bedroom. A male visitor volunteered to model how the apparatus works. He lay down on Jerry's bed on top of a special torso shaped sling. Peggy then wrapped and fastened the upper body part and then the legs part of the sling over the man and secured it to the lift.

Then with a push of a button the man was up, up and away being electronically transported on a ceiling track from the bedroom to the bathroom. There are two tracks on the ceiling. One carries the sling to the shower and the other goes to the commode area.

During the demonstration a precocious little boy moved in closer to take it all in. His eyes were bright with fascination over the whole procedure.

Peggy saw what was coming next when the little boy, about age six, asked for a turn.

Not wanting to disappoint the child but concerned for his safety, Peggy offered that the boy needed to get "a little bit bigger" before he could safely take a ride in the sling. This seemed to satisfy the boy and Peggy said, "You should have seen the look of relief on his Mother's face."

Beloved: "Come away, my lover, and be like a gazelle
Or like a young stag on the spice-laden mountains."
Song of Songs 8:14

Love Me Tender

The love this couple has for one another is palpable. It is a strong bond they see coming first as God's steadfast and unfathomable love for them that expands into a constant flow of receiving from and giving love back to God.

Not once in the years that I have been observing and befriending Peggy and Jerry have I ever witnessed this pair exchange harsh words. Perhaps a look of minor irritation that is short lived, but mutual respect is the rule.

These two share an intimacy that is something to treasure. Does that still include sex? Some people have a curiosity whether or not a handicapped person can function sexually. And, since this is a story about love it seems appropriate to give this delicate subject some consideration.

Some might assume that since they have seen Jerry in a wheelchair that the answer is probably no.

A few years back when the man with ALS could still sit in his wheelchair up to his computer table, I witnessed a little scenario taking place in the darkened corner of the room next to where Peggy and I were visiting.

From my vantage point, I could see that my husband, Jake, had pulled up a chair close to Jerry. He was hunched forward and the two men were looking intently at the computer screen. I assumed they were seeing recreational vehicles in some dealer's sales ads. Not so!

The men were ogling page-after-page of bikini clad women who had posed for the swimsuit edition of *"Sports Illustrated"* magazine.

Guys like to horse around and tease when they get together. Especially when they think no one is observing them. So, the next thing I heard my usually serious and proper husband ask his pal was how he could expect anyone to read a book about Jerry if it wasn't spiced up with a little s-e-x?

That question turned Jerry's face bright red.

It was a deep red.

It was purple red.

From the parlor, Peggy had cocked her head to hear what her husband might have to say, but Jerry wasn't talking. He likely figured he had said enough with the ever deepening blush that crept up his face.

Peggy just smiled and shook her head from side-to-side, as if to say 'boys will be boys' and returned her attention back to her guest.

It seems to me that Jerry has always been a strong male force to contend with and sex certainly is part of the vitality of any marriage, but we are not going to invade this dear couple's privacy even if it just might "spice up" this book.

A Minister's Comments

However, since it is important to the Weygandts that others faced with ALS receive encouragement to go on with their lives as best they can, I want to interject some thoughts on sexuality offered by a minister friend of mine whose husband died of ALS in 1995. She knew I was writing about a couple dealing with ALS and how their determination to face his deadly disease together had strengthened their marriage.

I had suggested to Marilyn (her name is changed to protect her privacy) that the Weygandts story was for all couples who face this disease with courage and grace.

In a private conversation at my home, Marilyn told me that ALS muscle deterioration does not take away from the person's skin to still have the sense of touch.

"If you continue to gently embrace and caress your husband and make love to him (he sees that) he is real again. That power is given back (to him)." The country parish pastor said.

The minister's personal experience with ALS has given her great compassion for those who must face this terminal illness. She sees marital sex as an important component to a loving couple's relationship and wants to assure others the need for tender love making can remain part of their lives right up to the dying partner's last days.

"Sex is a wonderful experience God has given us . . . it activates those feel good endorphins in your brain. God has made you to have this thrilling feeling and it is healing. It makes you feel loved and cared for, appreciated and desired," she told me.

"It's a miraculous experience. You feel refreshed and rejuvenated. My husband just beamed (with appreciation). It is good for both of you." The minister said.

And now, read on as the next two chapters illustrate some of the loving ways this amazing husband and wife have expressed love for their partner.

"Love each other as I have loved you."
John 15: 12

For the Love of Peggy

With the "windfall" Peggy started talking about taking a short vacation. "Just the three of us," she would say to her two best women friends.

Peggy realized it was now possible to consider taking time off for herself. The VA grant meant they could afford to hire a nurse's aide to stay with Jerry and he readily agreed and encouraged her to do it.

Since Jerry's progressively worsening illness, it had been years and years since Peggy had dared be away from him for more than an hour or so at any time. And, that meant a friend would come by and chat with Jerry while she quickly ran errands. She couldn't remember a time out to buy new clothes.

"My, what a difference the VA disabilities rating has made for us!" she enthused.

She told her friends, Amy Lingenfelter and me, Beverly Jacobson, to prepare for a special weekend to be held in early September of 2010. Peggy had gained confidence in the nurse's aide who was helping her care for Jerry.

After the idea for a "women only" weekend started germinating in Peggy, she would be fairly dancing a jig with excitement trying ideas out on the Wednesday lunch friends who would join her on the escapade.

She first thought about the trio staying in a Bed and Breakfast and tour Texas Hill Country. She did research on the computer almost every day came up with new options for the anticipated weekend. The biggest

94

attraction, however, turned out to be just a few miles from home. It was the new development called the Village of Fairview and the Village of Allen. Peggy and friends booked themselves for two nights into the Marriott Hotel. They had serious shopping to do at newly opened department stores like Macy's, Dillard's and JC Penney and dining at some great new restaurants.

The marathon spree left one friend shoeless and stretched out exhausted on a bed and the other, with bare feet up, sleepily reclining in a comfortable chair. That is how we watched while the avid shopper, Peggy, donned one new outfit after another.

"I don't know when I have had such a good time!" Peggy had enthused. "Maybe another time we can go see the wildflowers in the Hill Country!" We had sighed and smiled.

"Yes," we agreed, it would be fun to plan a trip to the Texas Hill Country.

Our sore feet were a small price to pay to see Peggy so elated.

Allen Community Outreach

The "windfall" also opened up a way for the couple to remember days when it had felt good to get all dressed up and go out for a romantic social evening.

For the first time in many, many years, they were able to wear party clothes and join friends at a table for eight to benefit the Allen Community Outreach program dedicated to helping the poor and needy in the Allen, Texas area.

"It felt great to enjoy a social night out like other people are able to do," said Peggy about the elegant evening they enjoyed at Heritage Ranch Country Club.

"When Jerry heard about it he said, 'Let's do it' and I quickly agreed," Peggy told her friend.

That night, she looked radiant in a purple beaded dress. The ensemble enhanced her silver hair and rosy cheeked complexion.

The paralyzed man said he was able to forget his disabilities and enjoy the evening "just like everybody else."

At the close of the evening, Jerry was overheard to say, "We had a wonderful time. I loved seeing my wife feeling pretty and special in a party dress!"

In fact, Jerry admitted to a special friend that he was so delighted by the happiness he saw on his wife Peggy's face at the ACO dinner that he decided to do something like that again.

Romantic Dinner at Baileys

Jerry had reservations made for them to celebrate their December 19th wedding anniversary with fine dining at the golden domed restaurant named Bailey's in the Fairview Village. Three other couples joined them for the evening. We sat warmed by a fire in the fire place at a table adorned with a beautiful centerpiece of red roses and the four women found floral wrist corsages at their places.

"It was good to be able to do this for my wonderful wife and our friends who have been so kind to us," said Jerry.

Those two special social events in spring and fall of 2010 were the last times Jerry and Peggy were able to enjoy an evening out.

"Where you go, I will go; where you lodge,
I will lodge; your people shall be my people,
and your God my God."
Ruth 1:15

For the Love of Jerry

The *"where you go, I will go"* Bible passage from The Book of Ruth was read at their wedding and it continues to be the theme of this marriage today.

In the Bible story, Ruth pledges to Naomi, her widowed mother-in-law, that she will follow her anywhere and will devote her life to her deceased husband's mother. This strong promise holds tremendous significance to Peggy as she dedicates her love and her life to Jerry. The Biblical Ruth was a strong and courageous woman who trusted and was guided by God. Like Ruth, Peggy is the strong and courageous woman who will do whatever it takes to love and care for Jerry.

"If the situation were reversed, he would be right there doing the same for me. He doesn't just have ALS . . . We do!" She told her writer friend.

"We—are—in—this—together!" she will tell you in a tone that sounds like a hammer striking a gong.

It has been her commitment ever since they recited their marriage vows.

She will never again be able to fall into the secure embrace of her once strong, vibrant, powerful husband. But while his body continues to wither away, their love grows. They have switched roles and this gentle little woman with a steel back bone has become her husband's fierce protector.

"I love him," she offers, simply.

"I miss his hugs."

Hospital Advocate

Throughout much of 2010 and into 2011, Peggy spent long hours with Jerry a frequent patient in area hospitals. (They chose not to have a signed 'DNR,' meaning do not resuscitate, directive regarding Jerry's care.)

From December—to-March, Jerry was rushed to a hospital eight times. It was not always the same medical facility because it depended upon Jerry's problem and the EMT's (Emergency Medical Technician) assessment of the patient's needs. The goal each time was for Jerry to improve enough to return home and receive Hospice supervised care; yet primarily from Peggy.

During this time, Peggy was overheard to fret because time was well past due to have their new van serviced. She had to cancel twice because of late night emergency trips to a hospital.

Finally, Jerry was stabilized. Peggy saw it as a chance to get the van serviced before her husband once again would return home for Hospice care.

Ever vigilant, it was Peggy's practice to be with her hospitalized husband from early morning until the close of visiting hours. She was not permitted to stay overnight because he was in intensive care. Thus, Peggy carefully explained to Jerry why he should not look for her to be at the hospital until the next afternoon.

The following day, after Peggy had taken time to get the van serviced, she found Jerry in a state of agitation; anxiously awaiting her arrival.

I had met Peggy in the hallway and followed her on her way inside the ICU to his room.

She saw that Jerry's food tray sat untouched.

She asked why he hadn't eaten.

"Did the hospital staff forget you?" (This had happened in a nursing home in an earlier time where Jerry was cared for while Peggy underwent gall bladder surgery.)

"No," he mouthed the word.

"Were they late?" she asked.

"No." he mouthed the word again.

"Was no one available to feed you?

His lips formed another "No!"

She looked puzzled for a moment.

"So, the food tray did come on time?" She asked.

"Yes." He mouthed the word.

"And an aide was here to feed you and you refused?"

"Yes." He mouthed the word.

She sighed.

She sat down her purse.

And, then she dutifully reached out her hand and lifted the spoon from the tray.

Jerry smiled and opened his mouth wide as the food approached his lips.

"But store up for yourselves treasures in heaven . . .
For where your treasure is, there your heart will be also."
Matthew 6:20-21

Advent 2010

By Advent Season of 2010, friends wondered if Jerry would see the New Year.

His blood sugar kept spiking. He had difficulty breathing. He had trouble swallowing. He told Peggy food just didn't taste good.

Numerous times, Peggy had begged Jerry to let the doctors' install a breathing tube and a feeding tube.

He continued to stubbornly refuse!

Peggy told me she thought her husband didn't want the breathing and feeding tubes because it was a sign that he was moving in to another sharp decline in this terminal illness and he did not want to face it.

She was right.

But, there was even more of a reason. Some months earlier on a visit to the house, I had found Jerry sitting up to his computer where he was watching a men's chorus sing *"How Great Thou Art."* He confided his secret desire was to sing once again with the church choir and this would be the hymn.

The breathing tube would make it impossible for him to speak or sing.

I felt sad to see my friend struggling mightily to hold on to life and his ambitious singing plan.

He was hospitalized several more times with breathing and eating problems, until he was finally forced to accept medical assistance or he would not survive.

I visited him in the hospital.

He looked glum.

He was no longer able to speak.

He could not breathe on his own power.

I touched his forehead and looked into his eyes.

"Do you still believe in God?" I asked.

"Do you still believe you are living out your spiritual purpose?"

Those intense eyes flashed angrily at me as if to say, that is a dumb or insulting question.

"Yes!" he moves his lips.

And, once again I was seeing Job in the ancient Bible story.

There is a Way

*J*erry felt a close connection and appreciation for his friend Bob Cochran who had been a faithful visitor during the numerous times Jerry was hospitalized as well as calling on him at his home.

But as springtime was in blossom, Jerry was back to home health care with Hospice and Bob was dead. Bob had not survived a surgery to repair an aneurysm. His funeral was set for May 23, 2011. Jerry was determined to go to honor his friend's memory.

And that's when David Franck, the Harmony Class dedicated teacher, was called to duty.

Since his retirement in 2000, David has been chief fixer and supervisor for just about any job needing to be done at the sprawling First United Methodist Church facility on Greenville Avenue in Allen where his wife serves as a pastor. The former HVAC (Heating, Ventilation and Air Conditioning) businessman is also credited with building and restoration projects for the Prothro Retreat Center, the North Texas Methodist Conference Center and the Bridgeport Children's Camp.

Jerry knew this about his Sunday teacher friend who occasionally accompanied his wife, Pastor June, on pastoral visits. So, it was a slam dunk as far as Jerry was concerned to call upon David to help the handicapped man attend his friend's memorial service.

It had been some time since Jerry had been out of bed. His last ambulance trip rushing him to a hospital was back in March. His illness had advanced so Jerry was hooked up to all sorts of medical equipment to keep him going. His high tech wheelchair sat empty outside his bedroom door.

One would think with all the paraphernalia needed just to stay alive it would dissuade Jerry from his quest to pay final respects to Bob Cochran.

Not so for Jerry! He is not one to shrink from a challenge.

Jerry needs to have a constant supply of oxygen, so he had dispatched Peggy on a quest to find a portable lightweight unit that would work on his wheelchair. They could not get one in time for Jerry to go to Bob's funeral. So, true to his way of thinking, Jerry just sought another way to make things happen.

That's when Mr. Fixit was called into service.

"I was asked if I could look into putting a battery pack on the Jerry Mobile," said David, in a telephone interview. He described a need for a particular plug to make it operable. After some trial and error David said he managed to get the mechanism rigged on the wheelchair.

"But, I had to take so much of the wheelchair apart to figure it out, I didn't think I could get it back together again." He joked.

After some trials, however, he did manage to get the wheelchair assembled and the plug mounted so it would provide proper voltage to the breathing machine. Peggy would not have to take along the heavy battery pack to provide oxygen for husband's outing to the funeral.

Success!" said David.

Jerry made it to the funeral, but came late and left early.

Sadly, he found that while the idea of attending his friend's memorial service was manageable in his mind, his body just could not withstand the challenges.

Shortly after surreptitiously positioning himself in the back row of the sanctuary, he mouthed words to tell Peggy that they would have to turn around and go back home.

Generator

Home was where we would find Jerry as we approached Christmas 2011. The days were sometimes gloomy, grey, and temperatures were dipping down into the thirties some nights. Winter rains were falling.

True to his Boy Scout nature to "Be Prepared" the man in bed had directed his wife to purchase a 4000 watt electricity generator. Here came Mr. Fixit again.

"They asked me to connect it to provide electricity for Jerry's medical equipment and the house in case of a power outage." David Franck later reported.

The challenge was to figure out how to make the proper connection using a 50 amp plug on the side of the house installed there for the motor home that had been sold.

"You cannot back feed your electrical system with a generator," David had explained to me because that would cause an electrical overload and blow out the Weygandt's electricity along with the entire neighborhood. But, one must assume that between the two men they safely worked out potential problems. There have been no reports of a power outage crashing an entire Plano neighborhood.

Peggy figured it was not so much out of concern over a possible power outage that the former electrician was inspired to want a portable generator as it was for him to go through the mental exercises to prove he could still see such a project through to completion.

When Peggy told me this story I thought back to my conversation about ALS with Marilyn, my pastor friend. She had told me that her ailing husband, totally immobile with the terminal illness, had convinced her that with his instructions she would be able to replace the clutch in her car. She proudly told me that she had accomplished just that following his step-by-step instructions. She explained that the person with ALS has nothing to do but keep his mind working. Such an exercise helps the person feel useful and proves they can still make a contribution. I believe Peggy would agree since many a time she would report going off on an unusual errand to fulfill yet another request from Jerry.

*"Arise! Shine, for your light has come
and the glory of the Lord rises upon you."*
Isaiah 60:1

Advent 2011

*A*nother year has gone by.
It is once again the Advent Season.

It is the festive time of year when Christians anticipate the birth of Jesus, the Christ Child and remember the rest of the story that by his death and resurrection we will have eternal life.

Peggy attends church alone. She joins the lunch bunch when she has someone to care for her beloved husband for several hours on a Sunday. Sometimes it is a Hospice nurse, other times it is family, Maureen and Lee Bowman.

Peggy tells me Jerry is ticking off things on his own kind of "bucket list" * of things he wants done before he dies.

His mind is busily planning the details for his own funeral. He has definite ideas of what pictures are to be shown, what music is to be played, the order of the service.

This has not been easy for my friend, but she complies because these are her "choiceless choices" . . . her mission is serving Jerry.

He has asked for Pastor June to come and pray for him . . . he wants a Methodist "last rites" sort of blessing. He wants to be assured that the book telling his and Peggy's love story, started four years ago, will see print. He wants to hold the book in his useless right hand.

His skin still has feeling so he may sense the weight of the book when the manuscript copy in a three ring binder is placed in his hand.

The "writers block" that seemed to haunt me in this project has lifted. It is as if I needed time in the past year to just let the subject "percolate" on some deeper level until the Holy Spirit was ready to guide my words. I needed my own spiritual deepening from the discipline of three years of study and exercise for a certificate in Spiritual Direction to prepare me for writing the love story of Jerry and Peggy . . . and God!

In November, 2011, I began to revisit what had previously been written. Now, when my hands touched the keyboard the words began to flow. I was guided!

I assure Peggy, "I am writing as fast as I can. Please tell Jerry to hold on; it soon will be Christmas!"

---

*Bucket List has become the popular term for out lining things one wants to accomplish before death, before you 'kick the bucket.' A movie titled "Bucket List" starred Morgan Freeman and Jack Nicholson.

"That joy is mine, it is now complete.
He must become greater, I must become less."
1John 3:29 & 30

How Great Thou Art

*J*erry lost his voice before he could realize the dream of singing one more time with the choir on a Sunday morning in church.

He had grandiose visions of soloing on *"How Great Thou Art"* with the church choir and orchestra.

Jerry had finally accepted that was not going to happen.

He has not been out of bed to go anyplace since last May's attempt to attend his friend, Bob Cochran's funeral.

But that has not stopped Jerry from imagining how it would be to sing this favorite hymn as a solo with magnificent accompaniment.

Where there's a will, there's a way.

And, Jerry's going straight to the top!

He now anticipates a Heavenly Choir; a host of angels, singing and playing harps. There will be a full orchestra; trumpets, bugles, drums, timpani, cymbals, bells, chimes, and lots and lots of violins!

And, there in the midst of this spectacular musical presentation will be Jerry. He will be boldly singing his heart out praising God as he makes his ascent into Heaven.

"Then sings my soul, my Savior, God to thee."
"How great thou art."
"How great thou art!"

It is Christmas.
Listen with your heart.
Can you hear Jerry singing?

"How great thou art!
How great thou art!"

Jerry and Peggy will tell you they believe their journey, their amazing love story is just beginning. They believe their story will go on and on because the best part awaits their reunion in Heaven!

And as Jerry would say, "The journey continues . . ."

Things I Would Like To Share With ALS Caregivers

By Peggy Weygandt

1) **Assume the role of caregiver.** You are now the advocate. Make sure your loved one is getting the best medical care possible. Your job is not to "play doctor," but to find the most competent and caring physicians you can. Work with medical professionals you can trust to guide you and your loved one through these difficult times. As you find strength you never knew you had, make sure you save some for your own life. Take time for yourself. One of the hazards of caretaking for an individual is sacrificing yourself in the process. Be patient with each other. Your loved one didn't ask to have ALS.

2) **Deal with one thing at a time.** Don't let ALS run your lives. During times of actual crisis, don't project or worry about the future. Deal with the immediate only. Pick out the closest goal or target. Don't begin to worry about what will or might occur down the road. Don't dwell on how traumatic these events are for everyone in the family. This will only increase your anxiety and distress. Pick the next step and place one foot in front of the other; concentrate fully on that. Your worry about the future is a waste of your energy during times of crisis. Furthermore, your predictions may be entirely erroneous. Work together. Don't try to do everything yourself.

3) **Acknowledge your emotional distress.** Fear is the most basic of emotions. When a loved one is ill or incapacitated, it can make you feel like a child again. Take the role of Caregiver. The fear of being alone rushes into your thoughts when we are reminded of our loved one's mortality. It is important to know that you will have moments of deep sadness and hopelessness when you see your loved one suffering, and that is a natural reaction. Tell your personal family doctor of your feelings and don't be afraid to take the medication that will help you through those depressing days and nights.

4) **Face your deepest fears and pain.** Most psychologists and spiritual leaders know the need to experience, rather than suppress these feelings. The completeness of death and fleeting quality of life are realities for us all. Knowing this from a spiritual perspective can help you speak of and deal with your intense feelings of your heart. This is not easy—but it is necessary and ultimately healing. Take and seek advice from your spiritual leader. They may not have gone through the same thing as you are going through or going to go through, but they are trained to help.

5) See the crisis as an opportunity for healing. Many individuals have had fractured and painful relationships with their parents or loved ones. Many spouses have left their loved one because this disease is so demanding on them. Seeing your loved ones as vulnerable, ill and wounded may offer new opportunities for healing. Rather than repeating this cycle of generational pain/anger, this can be a transformative time for all concerned. Look for ways to put the past behind you and be present, kind, patient and loving. Don't be ashamed of your loved one. Do not just close your doors and stay at home and wait for the inevitable. Take your loved one out among people. This helps them as much as it does you.

6) **Honor your loved one's spiritual journey**. Honor what is going on with your loved one on a spiritual level. In addition to the physical emergency, there is a higher truth. The physical brain/body is constantly changing and ultimately deteriorating. Remember that ALS is a degenerative disease. Spiritual forces will ultimately determine the outcome of this life, as well as its ending. This is not something you can control, although you can provide comfort, support, and care. Listen and watch for your loved one to give you a sign. Be in tune with your loved one and provide them with love, patience and kindness every day.

7) **Share your worries with others**. Don't try to deny your own pain and frustration. Find two or three good friends to confide your feelings in. Don't try to hold it in. It is important to find outlets to ventilate your own distress and tell the truth about what you are going through. Don't be afraid of frightening off others. Those who care deeply for you will be there for you.

8) **Experience the power of love.** Soak in the love. Let the love and prayers of others uplift you. On your journey, remember that love and prayers heals. Your presence in your loved one's life is a healing presence. Let others replenish you with their love and compassion along the way. Tell others that you love them and they will return the same.

9) **Let caretaking transform you.** When a loved one is in a crisis, we change our priorities and notions of what is important in our own life. The pursuit of material wealth, professional recognition, and personal gratification are easily shed. Unfortunately, after a while, time and again we forget these healing lessons and return to our prior state of awareness. Make an effort to allow the life teaching of caretaking to help you on the road to self-growth.

10) **Know when to let go.** When it comes to decisions regarding end of life or continued treatment, be sure to make the judgment based on the best interest of your loved one. Soon after your loved one is diagnosed with ALS sit down and make an Advanced Directive, Living Will, Medical Power of Attorney and you and your loved ones Last Will and Testament. Too often this is left until it is too late for the loved one to verbalize his/her wishes. Too often there are unnecessary tests, procedures, and surgeries performed on individuals who are in the process of actively dying and who have no realistic hope for recovery. Rather than allow relatives to die peacefully, some people "insist everything be done." This causes unnecessary pain and suffering, but with an Advanced Directive in place, all of your loved ones desire and requests will be carried out. Don't be selfish and let go in a timely fashion according to the Advanced Directive. You will know in your heart when it is time to let go and through the wishes of the loved one in the Advanced Directive.

11) **Take care of you, the caregiver.** This is the most important advice: Take care of your own physical, emotional, and spiritual needs. Those three things are most important. Physically take care of yourself as you will be the one to take care of your loved one.

12) **You will need both physical and mental strength** to be able to do that. Although we may be focused completely on our loved one's suffering, we need to be strong in order to be there for them. Withdraw

yourself mentally from the crisis for short periods of time, and do not feel guilty. Maintain good nutrition, exercise, even a half an hour a day, and rest as much as possible. Whether meditation, exercise, or prayer are your personal modes of finding strength, don't abandon them now. You have to be strong and mindful in order to help your loved one. I take time for myself in the grocery store while walking the aisles to reflect within myself.

Peggy referenced pamphlets and other printed material from the following agencies when she compiled the above list: Aspen Healthcare, Carestaf, Vista Hospice.

Edwards Brothers Malloy
Thorofare, NJ USA
April 30, 2012